The Zen of Digital Balance

The Zen of Digital Balance

Achieving Self-Discipline in the Tech Age

Ethan Ray

Mindful Pages

Published in 2023

ISBN: 9789358813708 (PB)
ISBN: 9789358814552 (eBook)

Published by

Mindful Pages
Imprint of Alpha Editions LLC
312 W. 2nd St #1834
Casper, WY 82601, USA

Contents

1

Understanding Our Digital World

In today's era, the digital world is not just a part of our lives; it has become ours. The advent of the internet, social media, and smart technology has reshaped how we communicate, work, learn, and even think. The pace at which digital technology has infiltrated every aspect of our existence is staggering, making it a defining feature of modern life. This integration has brought about unparalleled convenience and connectedness, but it has also ushered in a host of challenges that we are only beginning to understand and address.

The most profound impact of the digital revolution can be seen in the way we communicate. With the emergence of social media platforms like Facebook, Twitter, and Instagram, the world has become a global village. We can now connect with anyone, anywhere, at any time. This level of connectivity was unimaginable just a few decades ago. The benefits are evident; long-lost friends reunite, distant families can stay in touch, and professional networks expand beyond traditional boundaries. However, this hyper-connectivity has a flip side. It has led to the blurring of lines between work and personal life, as constant notifications and the pressure to be always 'on' take a toll on our mental health.

Moreover, the sheer volume of information available at our fingertips is both a blessing and a curse. The internet has democratized access to knowledge, making it possible for anyone with a connection to learn almost anything. But this abundance of information also leads to information overload. We are bombarded with news, opinions, advertisements, and content from multiple sources, often leading to confusion and the inability to focus on what truly matters. The skill of discerning valuable information from the trivial or false has become crucial, yet it's a skill that many are still developing.

Our relationship with digital devices, particularly smartphones, is another area of concern. These devices have become our constant companions, serving as gateways to the digital world. They are the first things we check in the morning and the last at night. While they offer immense utility, their overuse can lead to addiction-like symptoms. The dopamine hit from social media likes, messages, or new information keeps us returning for more, often at the expense of our real-world interactions and responsibilities.

The impact of digital technology on our professional lives is equally significant. The workplace has been transformed by digital tools and platforms, enabling greater flexibility, efficiency, and collaboration. Remote work, once a rarity, has become commonplace, largely thanks to digital advancements. However, this has also led to the erosion of work-life boundaries, with many employees finding it hard to disconnect from work. The expectation of being available 24/7, fueled by digital communication tools, has increased stress levels and burnout among professionals.

In the realm of education, digital technology has revolutionized how we learn and teach. Online courses, digital textbooks, and educational apps have made learning more accessible and personalized. Yet, this shift has also raised concerns about the quality of digital education and the potential for widening the digital divide. Students without reliable internet access or digital devices are at a disadvantage, highlighting the need for equitable access to digital resources.

Our leisure activities have not been immune to the influence of the digital world. Streaming services, video games, and online forums have changed how we entertain ourselves and socialize. While they offer new forms of engagement and community-building, they can also lead to a sedentary lifestyle and isolation from the physical world. The balance between digital leisure and physical, social activities is crucial for our overall well-being.

As we navigate this digital landscape, the question of privacy and security looms large. Our digital footprints are vast, with personal data being collected and often monetized by corporations. The implications for privacy are profound, and the debate around data protection and digital rights is ongoing.

Understanding our digital world is not just about acknowledging the presence of technology in our lives; it's about actively engaging with how it shapes our experiences, relationships, and perceptions. It's about finding balance in a world where the boundaries between online and offline are increasingly blurred. As we continue integrating digital technology into our lives, we must be mindful of its effects and take proactive steps to ensure that our digital experiences enhance, rather than detract from, our overall quality of life.

The journey through the digital landscape is complex, but it's a journey that we are all on together. By recognizing the challenges and embracing the opportunities, we can navigate this world with confidence and purpose, ensuring that our digital experiences are enriching and empowering.

The ubiquity of technology in the lives of adults

The ubiquity of technology in the lives of adults today is a phenomenon that has reshaped the fabric of both professional and personal spheres in profound ways. Technology is an integral part of our daily routines from the moment we wake up to when we go to bed. It has changed how we work and communicate and significantly influenced our personal lives, relationships, and leisure activities.

In the professional world, technology has revolutionized how we conduct business. The advent of high-speed internet, cloud computing, and mobile technology has made it possible for professionals to work from virtually anywhere. The traditional 9-to-5 workday in an office setting is no longer the only option; remote work and digital nomadism have become increasingly common. Tools like video conferencing, collaborative online platforms, and instant messaging have transformed workplace communication, making it faster and more efficient. Emails and digital documents have replaced paper, creating a more eco-friendly and organized work environment.

However, the pervasive use of technology in the workplace has also blurred the boundaries between work and personal life. The ability to be constantly connected means that the workday never really ends for some. Employees often find themselves checking work emails or completing tasks after hours, leading to increased stress and potential burnout. This 'always-on' culture, facilitated by technology, has raised questions about work-life balance and the long-term implications for mental health.

In the personal realm, technology has become deeply embedded in our daily lives. Smartphones, in particular, have become indispensable. They are not just communication devices; they are cameras, navigation aids, information sources, entertainment hubs, and digital wallets. Social media platforms have changed the way we socialize and stay in touch with friends and family. They allow us to share our lives with others and stay connected across distances. However, there is a growing concern about the impact of excessive social media use on mental health, particularly related to issues like anxiety, depression, and self-esteem.

Online shopping and digital financial services have also transformed how we manage our finances and purchases. The convenience of buying products and services online has led to a decline in traditional brick-and-mortar shopping and changed our consumption patterns. While this shift offers convenience and a wider selection of goods, it also raises concerns about data privacy and the security of online transactions.

Technology has also significantly influenced our leisure activities. Streaming services like Netflix and Spotify have changed the way we consume media, offering on-demand access to a vast array of content. Video games and virtual reality experiences provide new forms of entertainment that were unimaginable a few decades ago. However, the shift towards digital leisure activities has also led to a more sedentary lifestyle, which can have adverse effects on physical health.

The digital divide is another critical aspect of the ubiquity of technology. While many adults have access to the latest technological advancements, a significant portion of the population does not have access to reliable internet or modern digital devices. This divide creates disparities in access to information, opportunities for professional development, and participation in the digital economy.

Privacy and cybersecurity are other major concerns in our highly connected world. As we share more of our personal and professional lives online, the risk of data breaches and identity theft increases. The need for robust cybersecurity measures and awareness about digital privacy is more critical than ever.

The integration of technology into every aspect of adult life presents a paradox. On one hand, it offers unprecedented convenience, efficiency, and opportunities for connection. On the other, it brings challenges related to mental health, privacy, and the erosion of the boundary between work and personal life. Navigating this landscape requires a balanced approach, where we leverage the benefits of technology while being mindful of its pitfalls.

As we move forward, we must foster a digital culture that prioritizes well-being, privacy, and a healthy work-life balance. By doing so, we can ensure that technology continues to serve as a tool for enhancement and empowerment in both our professional and personal lives.

Blurring Boundaries: Work and Personal Life in the Digital Age

In the digital age, the once-clear lines between work and personal life have become increasingly blurred, a phenomenon significantly accelerated by the advent of new technologies. This 'always-on' culture, predominantly driven by constant connectivity, presents unique challenges in maintaining a healthy work-life balance.

The integration of technology into every aspect of our lives means that work can extend far beyond the traditional office space and hours. The accessibility of work emails and documents through smartphones and laptops has created a situation where employees are often expected to be available round-the-clock. This expectation to respond to work communications during evenings, weekends, and even vacations can lead to increased stress levels, burnout, and a decline in overall well-being.

Moreover, the rise of remote working, while offering flexibility and eliminating commute times, has further complicated the distinction between professional and personal time. Homes have transformed into offices, leading to difficulties in mentally 'switching off' from work. The absence of physical separation between work and home environments can make it challenging to establish clear boundaries, often resulting in work time bleeding into personal and family time.

This constant connectivity also affects personal relationships. The intrusion of work-related notifications into family meals, leisure activities, and intimate moments can strain relationships, as individuals may be physically present but mentally absorbed in work. This scenario can create feelings of neglect and frustration among family members and friends, impacting the quality of these relationships.

Furthermore, the 'always-on' culture can have adverse effects on physical health. Long hours spent in front of screens, lack of physical activity, and disrupted sleep patterns due to late-night work sessions can lead to a range of health issues, including eye strain, headaches, and chronic fatigue. The psychological effects, such as increased anxiety and reduced job satisfaction, can also be significant.

To combat these challenges, it is essential to establish clear boundaries between work and personal life. This might include setting specific work hours, designating work-free zones at home, and making conscious efforts to unplug from digital devices during personal time. Employers also play a crucial role by fostering a work culture that respects personal time and promotes a healthy balance.

In conclusion, while technology has brought numerous benefits to the professional world, its role in blurring the boundaries between work and personal life cannot be overlooked. Navigating this new terrain requires conscious efforts from both individuals and organizations to ensure that the integration of technology into our lives enhances rather than detracts from overall well-being and quality of life.

How the Digital World affects mental health and relationships.

The constant connection enabled by modern technology is a defining feature of contemporary life. While it has undoubtedly brought about significant benefits in terms of accessibility and convenience, its impact on mental health and relationships is a growing concern. This pervasive connectivity, facilitated mainly through smartphones and the internet, has reshaped the way individuals interact with the world and with each other, often with profound implications.

The Psychological Impact of Constant Connectivity

The human brain, while remarkably adaptable, is now subjected to unprecedented continuous stimulation. The barrage of notifications, emails, social media updates, and the expectation to be always available can lead to a state of chronic hyper-arousal. This constant state of alertness can result in increased levels of stress and anxiety. The brain's constant engagement with digital stimuli can interfere with its ability to process information and emotions effectively, leading to issues such as reduced attention spans, memory problems, and impaired decision-making.

The Paradox of Social Media

Social media platforms, designed to connect people, can ironically contribute to feelings of isolation and loneliness. While users can interact with a large network of friends and acquaintances, these interactions are often superficial. The curated nature of social media content can lead to unhealthy comparisons, with users feeling inadequate when measuring their real lives against the idealized versions presented online. This phenomenon, known as the 'comparison trap,' can exacerbate feelings of low self-esteem and depression.

Impact on Sleep and Relaxation

The constant presence of technology, particularly the use of screens before bedtime, can significantly disrupt sleep patterns. The blue light emitted by screens inhibits the production of melatonin, the hormone responsible for regulating sleep. Poor sleep quality, in turn, has a cascade of adverse effects on mental health, including heightened stress levels, mood swings, and cognitive impairments.

Work-Life Balance Disruptions

In the professional realm, the ability to be constantly connected has eroded the boundary between work and personal life. Employees often feel compelled to respond to work communications outside of regular working hours, leading to a sense of being unable to 'switch off.' This inability to disconnect can result in chronic stress, burnout, and a decline in job satisfaction, further affecting personal relationships and overall quality of life.

Digital Dependency and Its Consequences

The ease of access to information and entertainment through digital devices can lead to a form of dependency. This dependency can manifest as an inability to be alone or idle without resorting to digital devices for stimulation. The constant need for digital engagement can impair the ability to form deep, meaningful relationships, as real-life interactions often cannot compete with the instant gratification provided by digital content.

The Impact on Children and Family Dynamics

For families, the intrusion of constant connectivity can significantly alter dynamics. Parents absorbed in their devices can miss out on crucial interactions and bonding opportunities with their children. Similarly, children who are excessively engaged with technology may develop impaired social skills, struggle with attention issues, and experience delays in language and emotional development.

Mitigating the Effects of Constant Connectivity

Addressing the challenges posed by constant connectivity requires a multifaceted approach. Individuals can benefit from self-imposed boundaries on technology use, such as designated tech-free times and mindful consumption of digital content. Families can establish 'digital detox' periods to foster face-to-face interactions and strengthen relationships. Employers can play a role by promoting a healthy work-life balance and discouraging the expectation of constant availability.

The Role of Awareness and Education

Increasing awareness about the impact of technology on mental health and relationships is crucial. Educational initiatives can help individuals understand the importance of digital wellbeing and provide strategies for managing their digital lives. Mental health professionals can also offer support and guidance for those struggling with the adverse effects of constant connectivity.

The digital age has transformed the way we live, offering incredible opportunities for connection and access to information. However, it is vital to recognize and address the challenges it poses to mental health and relationships. By adopting a balanced approach to technology use, individuals can reap its benefits while mitigating its potential downsides.

The Unseen Hours

In the heart of Silicon Valley lived a software engineer named David. His life was a blend of code, coffee, and late-night emails. David loved his job, but as the lines between work and home blurred, so did the boundaries of his personal life.

David's day would begin with the chirp of his phone, pulling him from sleep into the world of emails and messages. Breakfast was often forgotten, replaced by quick glances at his laptop. He was a star in his company, known for his dedication and the uncanny ability to be always reachable, always on.

But this constant connectivity came at a cost. David's wife, Emma, longed for the evenings they used to spend talking about everything and nothing. She missed the spontaneous weekend getaways, now a distant memory overshadowed by David's unending work commitments. His ten-year-old son, Alex, had grown accustomed to his father's absence at soccer games and school events. David always promised to be their next time, a next time that never seemed to come.

One Saturday, David had promised to be home early to celebrate Alex's birthday. The house was buzzing with excitement, balloons, and laughter. But as hours passed, David was nowhere to be seen. He was trapped in another emergency at work, his fingers flying across his keyboard, oblivious to the ticking clock.

Finally, he arrived home, exhausted and drained, only to find a quiet house. The decorations were still up, but the party was over. Alex was asleep, his new football untouched. Emma's eyes, usually filled with understanding, now flickered with disappointment. It was a look that struck David deeper than any stressful workday.

That night, as he sat by Alex's bedside, watching him sleep, David realized what he had lost in the hours he had never seen. The small moments, the laughs, the hugs, the irreplaceable time with his family - all sacrificed at the altar of his online engagement.

Determined to change, David set new boundaries at work. He started leaving his laptop at the office, silencing his phone during family dinners, and dedicating weekends to his family. He began to rediscover the joy of being present, listening to Alex's endless stories about school, and seeing Emma's smile return.

As days turned into weeks, David found a new rhythm, a balance between his passion for work and his love for his family. He realized that being truly successful wasn't just about professional achievements but about being there for the moments that made life meaningful.

David's story reminds us of the delicate balance between our online and offline lives. In pursuing our careers, it's easy to overlook the moments that truly matter. But it's never too late to unplug, reconnect, and find our way back home.

2

The Price of Constant Connectivity

In the opening chapter of our exploration into the digital era's impact, we step into a world that is perpetually connected. This is the age of constant connectivity, a phenomenon that has swiftly transitioned from a novelty to a fundamental aspect of everyday life. The dawn of the internet, followed by the proliferation of smartphones and social media, has ushered us into an era where being online is not just an option but has become the norm. The digital age, marked by its immediacy and accessibility, has woven itself into the very fabric of modern society.

This constant connectivity has transformed the way we interact, work, and live. No longer confined to office desks or wired computers, the internet is in our pockets, on our wrists, and integrated into even the most mundane of daily objects. From the moment we wake up to the countless times we reflexively check our devices throughout the day, the digital world is a constant companion. It offers a stream of information, entertainment, and social interaction that is both exhilarating and overwhelming.

As we delve deeper into this chapter, we will explore the multifaceted consequences of this unceasing digital engagement. Our journey will uncover how the culture of being 'always online' has reshaped our psychological well-being, social interactions, and even our perception of the world. The digital era, while bringing the world closer in unprecedented ways, also presents unique challenges that we are only beginning to understand and address. This chapter sets the stage for a deeper understanding of what it means to live in a world where connectivity is continuous, examining both its marvels and its complexities.

Digital Fatigue

Digital fatigue, a relatively new phenomenon in our modern lexicon, is increasingly becoming a point of concern in the age of constant connectivity. As technology continues to permeate every facet of our lives, from personal interactions to professional engagements, the relentless exposure to digital screens and online content is taking a toll on both our mental and physical well-being.

Understanding Digital Fatigue

At its core, digital fatigue refers to a state of mental and physical exhaustion stemming from excessive use of digital devices such as smartphones, tablets, computers, and the consumption of digital content. This exhaustion is not merely a result of the time spent in front of screens but also from the way our brains process digital information. The constant barrage of notifications, emails, social media updates, and the never-ending stream of online content keeps our brains in a perpetual state of alertness, leading to fatigue.

Symptoms of Digital Fatigue

The symptoms of digital fatigue are diverse, affecting various aspects of our health and daily functioning. Mentally, it can manifest as a sense of burnout, difficulty concentrating, reduced cognitive capacity, and a general feeling of being overwhelmed. Physically, it may present as eye strain, headaches, disrupted sleep patterns, and overall lethargy. These symptoms can further exacerbate feelings of anxiety and stress, creating a vicious cycle of digital overconsumption and fatigue.

Causes of Digital Fatigue

One primary cause of digital fatigue is the sheer volume of information we are exposed to daily. Our brains are not designed to process the vast amounts of data we encounter in the digital world. This constant need to filter and process information can be mentally draining.

Another contributing factor is the blue light emitted by digital screens. This type of light is known to affect the body's circadian rhythms and disrupt sleep patterns, leading to fatigue. Additionally, the posture we adopt while using our devices, often hunched over a screen for extended periods, can cause physical strain and discomfort.

The social aspect of digital platforms also plays a role. The pressure to be constantly available and responsive on social media and professional networks can lead to a mental overload. The fear of missing out (FOMO) on important updates or engaging content can drive us to spend more time online, further fueling the cycle of fatigue.

The Consequences of Continuous Digital Exposure

Continuous exposure to digital content, especially without breaks, can diminish attention span and reduce productivity. The constant switching between tasks and platforms – a common practice in digital work and leisure activities – can overload the brain, making it difficult to focus and process information efficiently.

Moreover, digital fatigue can spill over into our personal lives, affecting our ability to engage in meaningful face-to-face interactions and participate in non-digital activities. Over time, this can lead to a deterioration in personal relationships and a decrease in overall life satisfaction.

Addressing Digital Fatigue

Combating digital fatigue requires conscious effort and changes in digital habits. This can include setting specific times for using digital devices, taking regular breaks from screens, and engaging in activities that do not involve digital technology. Practising good screen hygiene, such as adjusting screen brightness, using blue light filters, and maintaining proper posture, can also mitigate the physical symptoms of digital fatigue.

Understanding and addressing digital fatigue is crucial as we navigate this digital-dominated era. By recognizing the signs and taking proactive steps to manage our digital consumption, we can preserve our mental and physical health, ensuring that our use of technology remains a positive force in our lives.

Impact on Real-Life Relationships

The digital era has radically transformed how we interact and maintain relationships, ushering in an age of heightened connectivity. However, this constant online engagement has paradoxical effects on real-life relationships. While digital platforms have made it easier to stay in touch with distant friends and relatives, they have also introduced challenges that can lead to feelings of isolation and a decline in the quality of face-to-face interactions.

The Paradox of Digital Connectivity

The ability to connect instantly with anyone, anywhere, is one of the defining features of modern communication technology. Social media platforms, messaging apps, and video calls have bridged geographical distances and made maintaining relationships across long distances easier. However, this ease of connection comes with an unexpected twist: the more connected we are digitally, the more isolated we can feel in real life.

One explanation for this paradox lies in the nature of digital communication. Online interactions, often brief and superficial, lack the depth and emotional richness of in-person conversations. They miss out on non-verbal cues like body language, tone of voice, and physical touch, which are crucial for building strong emotional bonds. As a result, even with hundreds of friends or followers online, individuals can feel a sense of loneliness and disconnection.

Decline in Face-to-Face Interactions

The prevalence of digital communication has also led to a decline in face-to-face interactions. With the convenience of online chatting, the incentive to meet in person can diminish. This shift is especially noticeable among younger generations, who often prefer texting to talking. While digital communication is effective for sharing information quickly, it falls short in fostering deeper connections that are formed through shared experiences and in-person interactions.

Moreover, the habit of constantly checking phones even in the company of others – a phenomenon known as 'phubbing' – can be detrimental to building and maintaining strong personal relationships. This behavior can make the people we are physically with feel ignored, undervalued, and frustrated, leading to conflicts and a sense of emotional distance.

Impact on Romantic Relationships

In romantic relationships, the impact of constant online engagement can be particularly pronounced. Online distractions can lead to a lack of presence and attention in moments that are important for building intimacy. The use of social media can also bring about issues of trust and jealousy, with partners feeling insecure about online interactions with others.

The Influence on Family Dynamics

Family dynamics, too, are not immune to the influences of constant connectivity. Parents may find themselves competing with screens for their children's attention, while children might feel neglected when their parents are absorbed in their devices. These scenarios can lead to a breakdown in communication and emotional disconnect within the family.

Rekindling Real-Life Connections

To mitigate the effects of digital overuse on relationships, it is essential to prioritize face-to-face interactions. Setting aside technology-free time during family meals, social gatherings, and dates can help foster a sense of presence and attentiveness. Encouraging open conversations about the impact of technology on relationships can also be beneficial.

Furthermore, using technology to facilitate rather than replace in-person interactions can help maintain a healthy balance. For instance, video calls can be used to stay connected with long-distance family and friends, but efforts should be made to meet in person when possible.

The digital age has redefined the landscape of human interaction, presenting both opportunities and challenges for personal relationships. While technology has the power to connect us across vast distances, it is crucial to recognize its limitations in cultivating deep, meaningful connections. Balancing online engagement with a conscious effort to nurture real-life relationships is key to ensuring that our digital lives enhance rather than detract from our human connections.

The Illusion of Multitasking

The digital age has heralded an era of unprecedented connectivity and access to information, bringing with it the notion that multitasking is not only possible but also an efficient way to manage our digital lives. However, this perception often stands on shaky ground. The concept of multitasking, especially in the context of handling multiple digital tasks, is more of an illusion than a reality, with several studies debunking its supposed efficiency.

The Myth of Multitasking

Multitasking, in the traditional sense, implies the ability to perform several tasks simultaneously. In the digital realm, this often translates to switching between different applications, responding to emails while attending virtual meetings, or browsing social media while working on a project. The common belief is that this approach leads to increased productivity; however, the truth is quite the contrary.

Research in cognitive science consistently shows that the human brain is not wired to handle multiple tasks at the same level of efficiency and effectiveness as it does single tasks. When we think we are multitasking, we are actually rapidly shifting our focus from one task to another. This constant switching comes with a cognitive cost, known as the "switching cost." Every time we move from one activity to another, the brain has to reorient itself, leading to a loss of focus, efficiency, and ultimately, a decrease in productivity.

Impact on Productivity

The illusion of multitasking in the digital age can significantly hamper productivity. Tasks that could be completed efficiently if handled individually often take longer when intermingled with other activities. This is due to the splitting of attention, which prevents individuals from fully engaging with any single task. The quality of work can also suffer, as the depth of understanding and attention to detail are compromised.

Furthermore, this constant task-switching can lead to a build-up of cognitive fatigue, making it harder to focus and process information as the day progresses. This fatigue not only affects work-related tasks but also spills over into personal life, impacting our ability to engage in leisure activities and social interactions effectively.

Increased Stress Levels

Attempting to juggle multiple digital tasks can lead to heightened stress levels. The pressure to respond instantly to every email, message, or notification creates a sense of urgency and anxiety, contributing to a stressful work environment. This constant state of high alert can lead to feelings of overwhelm and burnout.

Moreover, the inability to complete tasks efficiently due to divided attention can contribute to a sense of inadequacy and frustration. In the long term, this can affect an individual's self-esteem and job satisfaction, further exacerbating stress and anxiety.

The Way Forward

Acknowledging the pitfalls of multitasking in the digital age is the first step towards more efficient work habits. Focusing on one task at a time, known as 'single-tasking,' can significantly boost productivity and reduce stress levels. This approach allows for deeper concentration, leading to higher quality work and faster completion of tasks.

Implementing practical strategies such as designated times for checking emails, using website blockers during work hours, and setting clear boundaries between different tasks can help foster a more focused and less stressful work environment. Additionally, taking regular breaks to rest the mind and avoid cognitive overload is crucial.

The allure of multitasking in our digital lives is strong, but understanding its limitations is key to maintaining productivity and mental well-being. By embracing single-tasking and consciously managing our digital activities, we can navigate the digital world more efficiently and with less stress.

Sleep Disruption and Health Issues

The pervasive nature of technology in our daily lives, particularly our constant connectivity, has introduced a range of health concerns, chief among them being the disruption of sleep patterns. The use of digital devices, especially before bedtime, is increasingly recognized as a significant factor contributing to sleep disturbances and associated health issues.

The Impact of Blue Light on Sleep

One of the primary ways in which technology affects sleep is through the emission of blue light from screens. Blue light, which is also present in daylight, plays a crucial role in regulating our circadian rhythms, or the body's natural sleep-wake cycle. Exposure to blue light during the day helps maintain a healthy circadian rhythm. However, exposure to it at night – which occurs when using smartphones, tablets, computers, or watching television – can disrupt this cycle. The blue light tricks the brain into thinking it's still daytime, reducing the production of melatonin, the hormone responsible for sleepiness, and thereby making it harder to fall asleep.

Digital Distractions and Sleep Latency

Apart from the physiological effects of blue light, the very nature of constant connectivity can also impede the ability to fall asleep. Engaging with digital content, whether it's scrolling through social media, replying to emails, or reading news, can keep the mind active and alert, making it more difficult to wind down and relax before bedtime. This constant engagement increases sleep latency, the time it takes to fall asleep after going to bed.

The Link Between Connectivity and Sleep Quality

Even when individuals manage to fall asleep after using digital devices, the quality of sleep can be compromised. Notifications from phones or tablets can cause disruptions, fragmenting sleep and reducing its restorative quality. Frequent awakenings due to digital notifications can lead to sleep fragmentation, which is associated with daytime drowsiness, impaired cognitive function, and mood disturbances.

Health Consequences of Poor Sleep

The consequences of disrupted sleep patterns extend beyond mere tiredness. Chronic sleep deprivation is linked to a range of health issues, including obesity, type 2 diabetes, cardiovascular disease, and weakened immune function. Furthermore, poor sleep quality is associated with mental health problems, such as increased susceptibility to stress, anxiety, and depression.

Strategies for Minimizing Technology's Impact on Sleep

To mitigate the impact of technology on sleep, it is essential to adopt healthier digital habits, particularly in the evening. Establishing a digital curfew, where electronic devices are turned off or set aside an hour or two before bedtime, can be highly beneficial. Creating a bedtime routine that promotes relaxation, such as reading a book, meditating, or taking a bath, can also help prepare the body and mind for sleep.

The use of night mode settings on devices, which reduce blue light emission, is another way to lessen the impact on sleep. Additionally, keeping digital devices out of the bedroom can minimize the temptation to engage with them before sleep and reduce sleep disruptions from notifications.

Embracing Technology Responsibly for Better Sleep

In our digitally connected world, it is vital to recognize and address the impact of technology on our sleep and overall health. By understanding the ways in which constant connectivity affects our sleep patterns and adopting measures to counteract these effects, we can enjoy the benefits of technology without compromising our sleep quality and health. Embracing technology responsibly is key to maintaining a healthy balance in our digital lives.

The Digital Workplace

The advent of the digital age has revolutionized the workplace, bringing with it a host of benefits, such as increased flexibility and connectivity. However, this transformation has also introduced significant challenges, particularly regarding the expectation of constant online presence in a professional context. This 'always-on' culture, fueled by digital advancements, has far-reaching implications for employees' work-life balance and overall well-being.

The 'Always-On' Culture in the Digital Workplace

The digital workplace has blurred the traditional boundaries between the office and home. With the advent of smartphones, laptops, and cloud computing, employees can access work-related tasks and communication anywhere and anytime. This shift towards an 'always-on' culture means that the distinction between work hours and personal time has become increasingly vague.

Employees often feel the pressure to respond to work emails, messages, and calls outside of standard working hours, including evenings, weekends, and even during vacations. This expectation to be perpetually available can lead to a sense of never truly being 'off the clock,' contributing to prolonged work hours and encroachment into personal time.

Impact on Work-Life Balance

The consequence of this always-on culture is a significant strain on work-life balance. The inability to disconnect from work can lead to a scenario where professional responsibilities perpetually overshadow personal life. Family time, personal hobbies, and relaxation periods are frequently interrupted by work demands, leading to employees feeling they are living at work rather than working to live.

This erosion of boundaries can have profound psychological and physical implications. Constant engagement with work-related tasks leaves little room for personal rejuvenation, leading to increased stress, burnout, and in some cases, mental health issues like anxiety and depression.

Reduced Productivity and Job Satisfaction

Ironically, the expectation to be always online can also negatively impact productivity and job satisfaction. The quality of work can suffer when employees are overworked and stressed. Continuous work without adequate breaks can lead to decreased creativity, diminished concentration, and an overall reduction in output quality.

Moreover, the lack of a clear separation between work and personal life can lead to job dissatisfaction. Employees who struggle to maintain a healthy balance are more likely to experience feelings of resentment towards their job, potentially leading to higher turnover rates and a decline in morale within the workplace.

The Need for Digital Boundaries

Addressing the challenges posed by the digital workplace requires the establishment of clear digital boundaries. Companies need to foster a culture that respects personal time and recognizes the importance of disengaging from work to maintain employee well-being. This could involve implementing policies that discourage after-hours communication or setting specific 'offline' periods where employees are not expected to respond to work-related messages.

Encouraging Mindful Use of Technology

Creating a healthy digital workplace also involves encouraging employees to engage in mindful use of technology. This includes being aware of one's digital habits and actively making choices that promote a healthy balance. It could involve simple actions like turning off email notifications outside of work hours or dedicating specific times to check emails rather than constantly throughout the day.

With its blend of flexibility and constant connectivity, the digital workplace presents opportunities and challenges. While it offers unprecedented access to work resources, it also poses risks to work-life balance and employee well-being. Navigating this landscape requires a conscious effort from employers and employees to create a working environment that values and respects the need for personal time and space, ensuring that the digital tools designed to facilitate work do not dominate our lives.

Coping Strategies

As we navigate the complexities of a digitally-dominated world, developing strategies to mitigate the adverse effects of constant connectivity is imperative. While technology has brought numerous benefits, maintaining a balance is crucial for our mental and physical well-being. This conclusion offers practical advice on establishing digital boundaries, undergoing digital detoxes, and prioritizing face-to-face interactions to foster a healthier relationship with technology.

Establishing Digital Boundaries

One of the most effective ways to counteract the drawbacks of constant connectivity is to set clear digital boundaries. This means defining specific times and spaces where digital device use is limited or prohibited. For instance, making bedrooms a no-device zone can help improve sleep quality and promote relaxation. Similarly, setting aside specific times of the day as 'offline periods,' such as during meals or family time, can enhance the quality of personal interactions and reduce the urge to check digital devices constantly.

The Role of Digital Detox

A digital detox, or a time when one refrains from using electronic devices, can be incredibly beneficial. This doesn't have to be a long or extreme process; even a short break can provide significant benefits. For example, dedicating weekends or certain hours of the day to being device-free can help reset one's digital habits. A digital detox helps gain perspective on the amount of time and energy spent online, leading to a more mindful use of technology.

Prioritizing Face-to-Face Interactions

In an era where digital communication is the norm, prioritizing face-to-face interactions can profoundly impact our well-being. Direct personal interactions strengthen relationships, enhance empathy, and improve communication skills. It's essential to make a conscious effort to spend time with friends and family without the interference of digital devices. This can involve activities like group meals, outdoor activities, or simply having conversations where digital devices are out of sight.

Mindful Use of Technology

Being mindful about how and why we use digital technology is key to managing its impact on our lives. This involves awareness of our digital habits and their effects on our mental health and relationships. It's helpful to assess our digital consumption and regularly adjust as needed. For instance, unfollowing or muting social media accounts that cause stress or anxiety can lead to a more positive online experience.

Setting Realistic Expectations at Work

In the professional realm, it's essential to set realistic expectations regarding availability and response times. Communicating with colleagues and superiors about digital boundaries can help manage work-related stress. This might include defining times for checking and responding to work emails or messages.

While the digital age offers unprecedented opportunities for connectivity and access to information, it's crucial to thoughtfully manage its impact on our lives. By setting digital boundaries, periodically detoxing from digital devices, prioritizing real-life interactions, and being mindful of our digital consumption, we can enjoy the benefits of technology without letting it overpower our well-being. As we become more conscious of our digital habits, we can navigate the digital world in a healthy, balanced, and beneficial way to our overall quality of life.

3

Rediscovering the Joy of Offline Life

As we turn the pages of our increasingly digital lives, this chapter invites us to explore the vibrant world beyond our screens. This chapter celebrates the rich, multifaceted experiences that await us when we step away from our digital devices and immerse ourselves in the physical world. It's about reconnecting with the fundamental aspects of life that technology, for all its advancements, cannot replicate.

This exploration delves into the myriad activities and interactions that make our lives fuller and more meaningful. We'll discover how engaging with people face-to-face, indulging in physical activities, and immersing ourselves in hobbies and pursuits that don't involve screens can profoundly enrich our existence. This chapter is not just about the absence of technology but about the presence of something more tangible, authentic, and often more fulfilling.

Through this journey, we aim to rekindle our appreciation for offline life's simple yet profound joys. We'll explore how these activities nourish our souls, enhance our well-being, and bring us closer to our true selves and to others. Whether it's the laughter shared in a physical gathering, the sense of accomplishment in a hands-on project, or the peace in a quiet moment away from the digital buzz, this chapter celebrates them all.

"Rediscovering the Joy of Offline Life" is an invitation to pause, reflect, and actively engage in the world in its most natural form. It's a guide to finding balance in an increasingly digital age, reminding us that sometimes the best way to move forward is to step back from the online world and embrace the tangible joys around us.

Mental Health Benefits of Offline Activities

In an age where digital devices dominate much of our daily lives, the value of offline activities has become increasingly significant, particularly regarding mental health. While the benefits of technology are manifold, it is equally important to recognize the mental health advantages that arise from engaging in offline activities. Activities such as spending time in nature, practising mindfulness, indulging in hobbies, or simply enjoying moments of disconnection can profoundly impact our psychological well-being.

The Therapeutic Power of Nature

Spending time in nature is one of the most effective offline activities for improving mental health. The natural environment has a unique ability to enhance psychological well-being. Studies have shown that time spent in green spaces, such as parks, forests, and beaches, can significantly reduce stress, anxiety, and depression. This phenomenon, often called 'eco-therapy', involves immersing oneself in the natural world, allowing the mind to relax and rejuvenate.

Nature's impact on mental health can be attributed to several factors. The calming effect of natural landscapes, the soothing sounds of wildlife, and the fresh, clean air all contribute to peace and tranquility. Furthermore, activities such as hiking, gardening, or simply walking in a park can also provide physical exercise, a known mood booster.

Mindfulness and Meditation

Mindfulness and meditation are other offline practices with substantial benefits for mental health. These practices involve focusing on the present moment, acknowledging and accepting one's feelings, thoughts, and bodily sensations. Regular mindfulness practice has been shown to reduce symptoms of anxiety and depression, improve attention and concentration, and enhance overall emotional regulation.

The beauty of mindfulness is that it can be practised anywhere, anytime, without digital devices. Simple exercises such as deep breathing, body scans, or mindful observation can be incorporated into daily routines, offering a respite from the constant bombardment of digital information.

Engaging in Offline Hobbies

Participation in offline hobbies is another way to improve mental health. Activities such as reading, painting, cooking, or playing a musical instrument provide an outlet for creativity and self-expression. These hobbies can act as a form of therapy, offering an escape from everyday stresses and a way to process emotions constructively and enjoyably.

Engaging in hobbies also provides learning and personal growth opportunities, leading to feelings of accomplishment and increased self-esteem. The focus required in these activities can also serve as mindfulness, keeping the practitioner engaged in the present moment and away from digital distractions.

The Joy of Disconnection

The simple act of disconnecting from digital devices can have a surprisingly positive effect on mental health. Reducing screen time, especially from social media and news websites, can decrease feelings of anxiety and envy and improve mood and self-esteem. Disconnection allows for more meaningful engagement with the physical world and promotes healthier sleep patterns, further enhancing mental well-being.

Social Interactions and Relationships

Offline activities often involve social interactions, which are crucial for mental health. Engaging in group activities, such as team sports, book clubs, or community volunteering, can build a sense of belonging and provide social support, both of which are key factors in maintaining good mental health. Face-to-face interactions have a depth and authenticity that digital communication often lacks, allowing for stronger connections and a greater sense of community.

While the digital world offers many conveniences and advantages, balancing online activities with offline experiences is crucial. Engaging in activities such as leisure time in nature, practising mindfulness, hobbies, and disconnecting from digital devices can significantly improve mental health, reduce stress, and enhance overall well-being. These activities provide a much-needed break from the digital world, offering relaxation, self-expression, and genuine social connection opportunities. As we navigate our increasingly digital lives, it's important to remember the value of stepping away from the screen and experiencing the world in its most natural, unfiltered form.

Strengthening Personal Relationships

In an era where digital communication is pervasive, the importance of offline interactions in strengthening personal relationships cannot be overstated. While technology has made staying in touch easier, face-to-face interactions truly deepen and fortify the bonds we share with friends and family.

The Essence of Face-to-Face Communication

Face-to-face communication is the cornerstone of strong, healthy relationships. Unlike digital communication, it encompasses not just words but also tone of voice, body language, facial expressions, and physical touch. These non-verbal cues are integral to fully understanding and connecting with another person. They convey emotions and intentions in a way that text messages or emails cannot, allowing for a richer, more nuanced form of communication.

When we interact in person, we are fully present in the moment. This presence fosters more profound empathy and understanding as we are more attuned to the other person's feelings and reactions. Face-to-face conversations often lead to more meaningful discussions, allowing for the sharing of experiences, emotions, and vulnerabilities in a safe and supportive environment.

Ethan Ray

Building Trust and Connection

Offline interactions are pivotal in building trust, a fundamental element in any relationship. Trust is cultivated over time through shared experiences and consistent, reliable behaviours – aspects that are more effectively communicated and perceived in person. In face-to-face interactions, it's easier to grasp sincerity and genuineness, which foster trust and connection.

Physical presence also allows for the expression of affection through physical touch – a hug, a pat on the back, or a gentle touch on the arm. These small gestures can communicate care and support in ways that words alone cannot, further strengthening the emotional bond between individuals.

Quality Time and Shared Experiences

Spending quality time together is another vital aspect of strengthening personal relationships, and it is most effectively done offline. Engaging in shared activities, whether a family meal, a walk in the park, or a board game night, creates memories and experiences that form the foundation of solid relationships. These activities provide opportunities for laughter, joy, and sometimes even challenges that, when navigated together, strengthen the bond between individuals.

Overcoming Digital Barriers

In today's digital world, it's easy to fall into the trap of believing that liking a post or sending a quick text is enough to maintain a relationship. However, these digital interactions often lack depth and personal touch. Taking the time to meet someone in person, to listen to them, and to engage with them fully shows a level of commitment and care that far exceeds any form of digital communication.

Nurturing Relationships Across Distances

While face-to-face interaction is ideal, it's not always possible, especially in long-distance relationships. In these cases, prioritizing periodic in-person visits can have a profound impact. When physical presence isn't feasible, using technology to approximate face-to-face interactions – such as video calls – can also help maintain the connection.

While the digital world offers convenience and a certain level of connectivity, offline interactions truly nurture and deepen personal relationships. The quality of communication, emotional depth, and genuine connection achieved through face-to-face interactions are unparalleled. As we navigate our increasingly digital lives, it's essential to consciously prioritize in-person connections, recognizing their irreplaceable value in fostering solid and enduring relationships.

Physical Health and Outdoor Activities

In an age where screens often dominate our daily routines, the significance of physical health and outdoor activities has never been more pronounced. Engaging in outdoor activities and sports is a leisurely pursuit and a fundamental aspect of maintaining overall health and well-being. These activities provide a necessary and refreshing counterbalance to our increasingly digital lifestyles.

The Physical Benefits of Outdoor Activities

The physical health benefits of engaging in outdoor activities are extensive. Activities such as hiking, cycling, swimming, or playing sports like soccer and basketball are excellent forms of aerobic exercise that improve cardiovascular health. Regular participation in these activities reduces the risk of chronic diseases such as heart disease, hypertension, and diabetes.

Outdoor activities also play a crucial role in maintaining a healthy weight, improving muscle strength, and enhancing flexibility and balance. For example, rock climbing is an intense workout that builds muscle strength, while yoga in the park can improve flexibility and mental relaxation.

Mental Health Advantages

The benefits of outdoor activities extend beyond physical health, significantly impacting mental well-being. Natural settings provide a serene backdrop for physical exertion, offering a mental escape from the hustle and bustle of everyday life. Activities like jogging in a park or a beach volleyball game can be incredibly stress-relieving, helping to reduce anxiety and depression.

Being outdoors, especially in green spaces, has been shown to lower cortisol levels, a hormone associated with stress. The fresh air, natural light, and serene environment help rejuvenate the mind, offering a sense of peace and calm often elusive in our fast-paced, digital world.

Vitamin D and Sunlight

Outdoor activities expose us to natural sunlight, a vital Vitamin D. Vitamin D plays a significant role in bone health, immune function, and overall physical well-being. Regular exposure to sunlight during outdoor activities can help prevent Vitamin D deficiency, which is becoming increasingly common due to indoor lifestyles.

Social and Community Benefits

Engaging in outdoor activities often has a social component, whether playing team sports, joining a hiking group, or participating in community fitness classes. These social interactions benefit our mental health, providing opportunities for laughter, camaraderie, and building connections with others.

A Break from the Digital World

In a world where digital devices constantly surround us, outdoor activities offer a much-needed break. They provide an opportunity to disconnect from emails, social media, and the constant flow of information. This disconnection allows us to be present in the moment, enjoying the physical activity and the environment around us.

Encouraging an Active Lifestyle

Incorporating outdoor activities into our routine encourages a more active lifestyle. Simple changes, like walking or biking to work, taking stairs instead of elevators, or spending weekends outdoors, can make a significant difference. Families can encourage physical health by engaging in outdoor activities setting a foundation for a healthy lifestyle in children from a young age.

Outdoor activities and sports are essential for maintaining physical health, offering many benefits to our mental and emotional well-being. They provide a necessary respite from our screen-dominated lives, allowing us to reconnect with nature, our communities, and ourselves. In fostering an appreciation for the outdoors and encouraging regular physical activity, we pave the way for a healthier, more balanced lifestyle.

Mindfulness and Meditation

In our fast-paced, digitally-driven world, the ancient mindfulness and meditation practices have gained renewed importance. As we navigate a landscape saturated with digital stimuli, these practices offer a sanctuary for the mind, enabling us to disconnect from digital distractions and attain a state of mental clarity and peace. This section explores the significance of mindfulness and meditation in the modern context, highlighting how they can be instrumental in managing the challenges posed by our connected lives.

The Essence of Mindfulness and Meditation

At its core, mindfulness is the practice of being fully present in the moment, aware of where we are and what we're doing, without being overly reactive or overwhelmed by what's happening around us. Meditation, often used as a tool in mindfulness, involves techniques like focusing on the breath or a particular thought to achieve a mentally clear and emotionally calm state.

Ethan Ray

Counteracting Digital Overload

In an era where our senses are constantly bombarded by digital information – from endless social media feeds to incessant email notifications – our minds rarely get a chance to rest. This constant engagement can lead to mental exhaustion, known as digital fatigue. Mindfulness and meditation offer a way to counteract this overload. By grounding our attention in the present moment, these practices help quiet the mind, reducing the noise of the digital world.

Achieving Mental Clarity

One of the primary benefits of mindfulness and meditation is the attainment of mental clarity. Practising mindfulness, we learn to observe our thoughts and feelings without judgment. This observation creates space between our experiences and our reactions to them. Over time, this leads to a clearer, more focused mind, enhancing our ability to concentrate and make decisions.

Reducing Stress and Anxiety

Mindfulness and meditation are known for their stress-reducing properties. Engaging in these practices activates the body's relaxation response, a state of restfulness that is the polar opposite of the stress response. Regular exercise can lead to a reduction in everyday stress levels and a boost in feelings of joy and serenity. Additionally, mindfulness can help in managing anxiety, as it teaches us to anchor our thoughts in the present, preventing them from spiralling into anxious ruminations about the future.

Enhancing Emotional Well-being

Beyond reducing stress and anxiety, mindfulness and meditation can significantly enhance overall emotional well-being. These practices foster an increased awareness of our emotional state, helping us recognize and accept our feelings. This emotional awareness is crucial in developing healthier coping mechanisms and emotional responses.

Cultivating a Mindful Relationship with Technology

Mindfulness can also be applied directly to our use of technology. By becoming more aware of our digital habits, we can make more conscious choices about how we engage with technology. For example, we might decide to check our phones at specific times rather than constantly or to engage in a digital detox over the weekend. These mindful decisions about technology use can lead to a more balanced and less stressful relationship with our digital devices.

Practical Tips for Incorporating Mindfulness and Meditation

Incorporating mindfulness and meditation into daily life can be simple. It might involve setting aside a few minutes daily for meditation, practising deep breathing exercises during breaks, or even engaging in mindful walking or eating. The key is consistency and finding practices that fit your lifestyle and resonate with you.

Mindfulness and meditation offer powerful tools to navigate the complexities of the digital age. These practices foster a sense of inner peace and clarity by helping us disconnect from digital distractions and tune into our mental and emotional states. In our quest for a balanced life, mindfulness and meditation emerge not just as practices but as essential components of well-being in our increasingly connected world.

Practical Tips for Offline Engagement

In a world where digital devices are an integral part of our daily routine, finding time for offline engagement can sometimes feel daunting. However, integrating more offline activities into our lives is essential for maintaining a healthy balance. This section provides practical tips and actionable advice to help you incorporate more offline activities into your daily routine, enhancing your overall quality of life.

Ethan Ray

Setting Aside Specific Times for Hobbies

1. **Schedule Hobby Time**: Just as you would schedule a meeting or a doctor's appointment, set aside specific times in your calendar for hobbies. Whether it's an hour of reading, gardening, or painting, having it scheduled makes you more likely to commit to it.

2. **Limit Screen Time**: Allocate certain day hours as screen-free time. Use these periods to engage in hobbies that don't involve digital devices. This could be early morning hours or specific evenings each week.

3. **Create a Dedicated Space**: Designate a specific area in your home for your hobby. Setting up a space can motivate you to engage in your pursuit more regularly.

Planning Regular Meetups with Friends

1. **Initiate Recurring Social Events**: Establish a regular meetup with friends, such as a weekly dinner, a monthly book club, or a sports activity. Recurring events help create a routine and ensure consistent social interaction.

2. **Use Technology to Coordinate, Not Replace**: Utilize digital tools to plan and coordinate these meetups, but focus on face-to-face interaction during the event.

3. **Explore New Activities Together**: Trying new activities with friends can be a great way to strengthen bonds and create memorable experiences. Consider group classes, outdoor adventures, or local events.

Joining Local Clubs or Groups

1. **Find Local Clubs of Interest**: Look for clubs or groups in your area that align with your interests. This could be a hiking group, a gardening club, or a community art class. Local libraries, community centers, and online community boards can be great resources.

2. **Commit to Regular Attendance**: Try to attend regularly once you join a club or group. Consistent participation helps build connections and enhances the experience.

3. **Volunteer for Events or Activities**: Being actively involved, such as volunteering for events or taking on a role within the group, can enrich your experience and help you feel more connected.

General Tips for Offline Engagement

1. **Digital Detoxes**: Occasionally, have a digital detox day where you refrain from using digital devices. Use this time to engage in offline activities.

2. **Engage in Physical Activity**: Incorporate physical activities like walking, cycling, or yoga into your daily routine. These activities are good for your physical health and offer a break from digital screens.

3. **Cultivate Mindfulness**: Practice being present in the moment, whether having a meal, taking a walk, or spending time with loved ones. Mindfulness enhances the quality of offline experiences.

4. **Explore Nature**: Spend time outdoors. Activities like hiking, bird watching, or even a simple walk in the park can be incredibly rejuvenating and a great way to disconnect from the digital world.

5. **Embrace Boredom**: Allow yourself to experience moments of boredom without rushing to fill them with digital content. These moments can spark creativity and encourage you to explore new offline activities.

Incorporating offline activities into our daily lives is crucial for maintaining a balanced lifestyle. By consciously setting aside time for hobbies, regularly meeting up with friends, joining local groups, and embracing physical and mindful activities, we can effectively counteract the digital saturation of modern life. These practices enrich our lives and enhance our connections with the world, leading to greater fulfilment and well-being.

4

Strategies for Digital Detox

In this chapter, we embark on a critical journey towards reclaiming our time and mental space from digital overconsumption. This chapter is dedicated to unravelling practical and effective strategies for reducing digital dependency, an increasingly vital endeavour in our hyper-connected world. As we delve into this exploration, we aim to provide readers with the tools and insights necessary to initiate and sustain a meaningful digital detox.

Digital detox, the conscious reduction of technology use, is not just about stepping away from digital devices; it's about creating space for deeper connections with ourselves and the world around us. In a society where screens have become our constant companions, this chapter addresses the urgent need to pause and reflect on our digital habits and their impact on our lives.

Through a series of practical tips and techniques, we will guide you through setting specific times for unplugging, establishing tech-free zones, and integrating mindfulness practices into your daily routine. These strategies are designed as a temporary escape from the digital world and a stepping stone towards a more balanced and controlled relationship with technology.

From gradual reduction techniques to managing withdrawal symptoms, this chapter is a comprehensive guide for anyone looking to break free from the digital tether and experience life beyond the screen. Whether you're a social media enthusiast, a workaholic glued to your email, or simply someone seeking a respite from the digital noise, these strategies are tailored to help you achieve a healthier, more mindful digital existence.

"Strategies for Digital Detox" is more than just a chapter; it's a journey towards digital mindfulness and well-being. It's about learning to navigate the digital world with intention and purpose, ensuring that our interactions with technology are enriching, not depleting. So, let us embark on this journey together, discovering the joys and freedoms of a well-executed digital detox.

Self-Assessment and Goal Setting

The need for a digital detox has become increasingly apparent in today's digitized world, where our lives seem inextricably linked to our devices. However, the first step towards any form of digital or otherwise detoxification is self-assessment and goal setting. This section aims to guide you through the process of evaluating your digital habits and setting clear, achievable goals to reduce your digital footprint and enhance your overall well-being.

Understanding Your Digital Usage

The journey towards a successful digital detox begins with a thorough assessment of your current digital usage. This involves tracking how much time you spend on various devices and understanding the nature of this usage. Are you constantly checking emails, endlessly scrolling through social media feeds, or habitually engaging in online gaming? Recognizing these patterns is crucial in pinpointing areas that require change.

Reflective Questions for Self-Assessment

Start by asking yourself some reflective questions:

- How many hours a day do I spend on digital devices?

- What primary activities do I engage in online (social media, work, entertainment, news)?

- Do I feel anxious or uncomfortable when I cannot access my devices?

- Does digital usage interfere with my sleep, work, or personal relationships?

Tracking and Monitoring

Consider using digital tools designed to monitor screen time, which can provide insights into your digital habits. Many smartphones now have built-in screen time trackers that break down your usage by application and duration. This data can be eye-opening, offering a tangible metric to work from.

Setting Clear and Achievable Goals

Once you clearly understand your digital habits, setting achievable goals is next. These goals should be specific, measurable, and realistic, catering to your lifestyle and commitments.

- **Reducing Social Media Usage**: If social media consumes a significant portion of your day, set a daily limit. Start by reducing your usage by a certain percentage or setting specific times for social media.

- **Device-Free Time**: Implement device-free periods, such as during meals, one hour before bedtime, or the first hour after waking up. These times can help you reconnect with the offline world and improve sleep quality and interpersonal relationships.

- **Weekend Detox**: Designate one weekend a month as a digital detox period. Use this time to engage in offline activities like reading, hiking, or spending time with loved ones.

- **Work Email Boundaries**: Set boundaries for work-related communications. Decide not to check emails after a certain time in the evening or during weekends, if possible.

Revisiting and Revising Goals

As you progress, it's important to revisit and revise your goals. If you find a particular goal too challenging, adjust it to make it more attainable. Remember, the aim is to find a balance that works for you, not to adhere to a rigid set of rules.

Ethan Ray

Celebrating Milestones

Acknowledge and celebrate milestones in your digital detox journey. Recognizing your achievements can be highly motivating, whether it's a day without social media or a weekend digital detox.

Embarking on a digital detox journey through self-assessment and goal-setting is a powerful way to regain control over your digital life. Understanding your habits and setting targeted goals can significantly reduce your digital dependency, leading to enhanced mental clarity, improved relationships, and a more balanced life. Remember, the purpose of a digital detox isn't to eliminate digital usage but to create a healthier relationship with technology.

Gradual Reduction Techniques

In pursuing digital well-being, gradually reducing screen time often proves more sustainable and effective than an abrupt detox. Abrupt changes can be challenging to sustain and may lead to feelings of withdrawal or frustration. Instead, gradual reduction techniques can help ease the transition from excessive screen use, making the process more manageable and less overwhelming. This section outlines various strategies for slowly reducing screen time in a way that is both achievable and beneficial to your overall well-being.

Establishing a Baseline

Start by establishing a baseline of your current screen time. Use digital tools or screen time trackers to get an accurate picture of your time on your devices. Knowing your starting point is crucial in setting realistic goals for reduction.

Setting Incremental Goals

Once you have a baseline, set small, incremental goals for reducing your screen time. For example, if you spend three hours daily on social media, aim to reduce this time by 15-30 minutes each week. Gradual reduction helps your mind and body adapt to the changes without feeling deprived.

Scheduled Screen Time

Designate specific times of the day for using your devices. Schedule your screen time just as you would any other activity. Confining your digital activities to designated periods prevents the day from being consumed by aimless scrolling or unnecessary screen exposure.

Prioritize Activities

Identify the essential activities you perform on your devices and prioritize them. Determine which digital activities are necessary (like work emails) and which can be reduced (like social media or web browsing). Focusing on essential tasks can significantly cut down unnecessary screen time.

Tech-Free Zones

Create tech-free zones in your home where no devices are allowed, such as the dining room or bedroom. These zones encourage you to engage in other activities, like reading or conversing with family members, without the distraction of screens.

Substitute with Offline Activities

Find offline activities that you enjoy and substitute them for screen time. It could be something simple like taking a walk, practising a hobby, or reading a book. These activities reduce screen time and enrich your life with new experiences and skills.

Mindful Scrolling

Practice mindful scrolling when using social media or browsing the internet. Be aware of the time spent and the content you're consuming. Ask yourself whether this activity adds value to your life or is a habit. Mindful consumption can naturally reduce the time spent on these platforms.

Ethan Ray

Set App Limits

Most smartphones have features that allow you to set daily limits on specific apps. Utilize these features to limit time spent on the most time-consuming apps, such as social media or games.

Digital Sabbaticals

Experiment with short digital sabbaticals or breaks. Start with a few hours or a day without digital devices and gradually increase the duration. These breaks can be an eye-opening experience, showing how much you can accomplish without constant digital interference.

Monitor Progress and Adjust

Regularly monitor your progress and adjust your goals as needed. If a particular strategy isn't working, try a different approach. The key is to find what works best for you and to be flexible in your approach.

Reducing screen time is a practical and effective approach to achieving a healthier digital life. It's about making intentional choices regarding how and when to use digital devices. By implementing these strategies, you can enjoy the benefits of technology without letting it dominate your life. Remember, the goal is to create a balance that enhances, rather than detracts from, your overall quality of life.

Alternative Activities

Finding alternative activities is crucial in reducing screen time and embracing a healthier lifestyle. These activities substitute the time spent on digital devices and enrich our lives with new experiences and learning opportunities. The possibilities are vast and varied, from hobbies that stimulate creativity to physical exercises that boost well-being and social activities that enhance interpersonal connections. This section lists various engaging activities that can effectively replace screen time, offering a more fulfilling and balanced way of living.

Creative Hobbies

- **Painting and Drawing**: Unleash your creativity on canvas or paper. Painting and drawing are relaxing and great for expressing emotions and thoughts.

- **Crafting**: Try crafting activities like knitting, woodworking, or DIY home decor projects. Crafting can be a therapeutic and rewarding experience.

- **Writing**: Whether it's keeping a journal, writing poetry, or starting on that novel you've always wanted to write, writing is an excellent way to channel your thoughts and creativity.

- **Cooking and Baking**: Explore new recipes and experiment in the kitchen. Cooking and baking are not only enjoyable but also offer the reward of a delicious final product.

- **Gardening**: Gardening is a beautiful way to spend time outdoors. It's rewarding to see the fruits of your labor, whether in the form of flowers, herbs, or vegetables.

Physical Activities

- **Hiking and Walking**: Get outside and explore nature trails or walk in your neighborhood. Walking and hiking are great for physical fitness and mental relaxation.

- **Yoga and Meditation**: These practices improve flexibility and strength and help reduce stress and enhance mental clarity.

- **Cycling**: Whether it's leisurely bike rides through the park or more intense cycling, this activity is a great way to get exercise and enjoy the outdoors.

- **Dance**: Take a dance class or dance in your living room. Dancing is a fun way to stay active and can be a great social activity, too.

- **Team Sports**: Engage in team sports like basketball, soccer, or volleyball. They're a great way to stay fit and interact with others.

Social Activities

- **Book Clubs**: Join a book club or start one with friends. It's a great way to ensure you read regularly and provides an opportunity for insightful discussions.

- **Board Games and Puzzles**: Organize a game night with family or friends. Board games and puzzles are fun ways to challenge the brain and enjoy time with loved ones.

- **Volunteering**: Volunteering for a cause you care about can be fulfilling and a great way to connect with others in your community.

- **Attend Workshops or Classes**: Look for local workshops or classes in areas you're interested in, such as photography, pottery, or language classes.

- **Outdoor Adventures**: Plan outdoor group activities like camping, kayaking, or rock climbing. These adventures can be exhilarating and a great way to bond with friends and family.

Personal Development

- **Learning a New Skill**: Have you always wanted to learn to play an instrument or speak a new language? Now is the perfect time to start.

- **Reading**: Rediscover the joy of reading. Books can be wonderful companions, offering knowledge and escape from the everyday world.

- **Mindfulness and Relaxation**: Practice mindfulness or relaxation techniques like deep breathing or progressive muscle relaxation.

- **Exploring Art and Culture**: Visit museums art galleries, or attend a theater performance. Immersing yourself in art and culture can be a profoundly enriching experience.

Replacing screen time with these activities can lead to a more active, creative, and fulfilling life. Each activity offers unique benefits and the potential for new experiences and personal growth. By consciously engaging in these alternatives, you can break the cycle of excessive screen use and enjoy a more balanced and enriching lifestyle.

Managing Withdrawal Symptoms

In the process of reducing digital usage, it's not uncommon to experience withdrawal symptoms. These can range from restlessness and irritability to anxiety and a feeling of being disconnected. This reaction is natural, as our bodies and minds are accustomed to constant digital stimulation. Managing these symptoms effectively is critical to successfully transitioning to reduced screen time. This section provides advice on handling digital withdrawal symptoms and offers strategies to cope with them.

Recognize and Acknowledge the Symptoms

The first step in managing withdrawal symptoms is to recognize and acknowledge them. Common symptoms include:

- **Restlessness**: Feeling uneasy or fidgety without your digital devices.

Ethan Ray

- **Anxiety**: Worrying about missing out on updates or communications.

- **Irritability**: Feeling frustrated or short-tempered.

- **Mood Swings**: Experiencing rapid mood changes.

- **Difficulty Concentrating**: Finding it hard to focus without the constant stimulation from digital devices.

Understanding that these are normal responses to reducing screen time can help you cope with them more effectively.

Establish a Routine

Creating a structured daily routine can provide a sense of normalcy and control. Schedule your day with specific activities, mainly when using digital devices. Include time for work, physical exercise, hobbies, social interactions, and relaxation.

Practice Mindfulness and Relaxation Techniques

Mindfulness practices such as meditation, deep breathing, or progressive muscle relaxation can effectively manage anxiety and restlessness. These practices help bring your focus to the present moment and calm the mind.

Stay Socially Connected

Reducing digital use doesn't mean you have to cut off social interactions. Maintain a social life through face-to-face interactions. Spend time with family and friends or participate in group activities or clubs. Social support is crucial in dealing with withdrawal symptoms.

Find New Hobbies or Rediscover Old Ones

Engage in hobbies that don't involve screens. Whether it's reading, painting, gardening, or cooking, hobbies can be a great way to redirect your attention and energy. They can also provide a sense of accomplishment and satisfaction.

Set Realistic Goals

Be realistic in your approach to reducing screen time. Abrupt and drastic reductions can lead to more muscular withdrawal symptoms. Gradually decreasing your usage might result in milder symptoms that are easier to manage.

Digital Detox Before Bed

Make your bedroom a screen-free zone. Using digital devices before bed can disrupt sleep, and poor sleep can exacerbate withdrawal symptoms. Establishing a relaxing bedtime routine can aid in better sleep and overall mood.

Seek Support

If you're finding it challenging to manage withdrawal symptoms, don't hesitate to seek support. Talk to friends or family about what you're experiencing. Professional help, such as counseling or therapy, can also be beneficial, especially if symptoms significantly impact your daily life.

Be Patient and Kind to Yourself

Finally, be patient and kind to yourself during this transition. Recognize that managing withdrawal is a process, and it's okay to have challenging days. Celebrate your progress, no matter how small, and remember that each step forward is a step towards a healthier, more balanced digital life.

Managing digital withdrawal symptoms is an integral part of the journey towards reduced screen time. You can navigate this transition more smoothly by recognizing the signs, establishing routines, staying physically and socially active, and seeking support. Remember, the goal is to find a balance that enhances your well-being on and off the screen.

Technology itself can be a powerful ally in the quest for digital wellness. Surprisingly, certain apps and digital tools are designed to help monitor and limit screen time, which is crucial in aiding a digital detox. Additionally, creating a long-term digital wellness plan is essential for sustaining the benefits of a digital detox. This section will introduce some essential technology tools that aid in a digital detox and guide developing a sustainable digital wellness plan.

Technology Tools to Aid Detox

- **Screen Time Tracking Apps**: Apps like Moment, RescueTime, or Screen Time (built into iOS devices) help track your daily usage of various apps and websites. They provide detailed reports on how much time you spend on your devices, allowing you to identify usage patterns and potential problem areas.

- **App Blockers and Limiters**: Tools like Freedom, StayFocusd, or Cold Turkey allow you to block or limit time spent on specific apps or websites. You can set schedules for when certain apps are available, helping you avoid distractions during work hours or family time.

- **Focus and Productivity Apps**: Apps like Forest encourage focused work sessions by letting you plant a virtual tree that grows while you work and dies if you leave the app. Such tools help minimize the temptation to check your phone impulsively.

- **Wellness and Digital Balance Apps**: Google's Digital Wellbeing and Apple's Screen Time offer features to set daily screen time limits, bedtime modes, and Do Not Disturb settings, helping users manage their digital health.

Creating a Long-Term Digital Wellness Plan

- **Set Clear Objectives**: Based on the insights from your usage data, set clear and achievable objectives for your digital use. This could include reducing screen time, limiting social media use, or designating tech-free periods during the day.

- **Incorporate Daily Non-Digital Activities**: Ensure your daily routine includes activities that don't involve screens. This could be reading, exercising, cooking, or spending time in nature. These activities provide a break from screens and enrich your life in other ways.

- **Establish Tech-Free Zones**: Designate specific areas of your home, such as the bedroom or dining room, as tech-free zones. This can help encourage better sleep hygiene and more quality family time.

- **Regular Digital Detoxes**: Schedule regular digital detoxes - it could be a day each week or a weekend each month. Use this time to disconnect entirely from digital devices and engage in other fulfilling activities.

- **Mindful Usage**: Remember why and how you use your digital devices. Ask yourself if your current activity on the device is necessary or beneficial. Practising mindful usage can significantly reduce mindless scrolling.

- **Reassess and Adjust Regularly**: Review your digital wellness plan and adjust your goals as needed. As your lifestyle changes, your digital wellness plan may need to adapt.

- **Seek Support**: Share your digital wellness goals with friends or family so they can support you in your journey. Having a support system can make it easier to stick to your plan.

- **Celebrate Progress**: Acknowledge and celebrate your progress. Whether it's successfully having a tech-free day or reducing your social media usage, recognizing your achievements can motivate you to continue.

Leveraging technology tools to aid in a digital detox is an effective strategy to start regaining control over your digital life. Coupled with a well-thought-out digital wellness plan, these tools can help ensure long-term adherence to healthier digital habits. By conscientiously applying these strategies, you can enjoy the benefits of the digital world while maintaining a healthy, balanced life.

5

Cultivating Mindful Technology Use

This chapter delves into a crucial aspect of our modern lives – how we interact with technology. This chapter is not just about reducing screen time; it's about transforming our relationship with digital devices and the internet. In a world where technology is ubiquitous, affecting almost every aspect of our daily lives, we must approach our digital habits with mindfulness and intention.

The dawn of the digital age has brought about remarkable advancements. Technology has connected us across continents, streamlined our work, provided endless sources of information and entertainment, and in many ways, made our lives easier and more efficient. However, as with any significant change, this comes with its challenges. The convenience of constant connectivity has led to a culture of perpetual digital engagement, where the lines between useful interaction and compulsive use are often blurred.

Mindful technology use is about creating a harmonious relationship with our digital devices – one where we are in control, and our usage is purposeful and intentional. It's about using technology as a tool to enhance our lives rather than as a means of escapism or mindless consumption. This chapter aims to teach readers the art of mindful technology use, guiding them through the process of becoming more aware of their digital habits and learning to use technology in a way that is beneficial to their mental and emotional well-being.

The journey towards mindful technology use starts with understanding our current relationship with our devices. It involves observing our habits – the reflexive checking of phones, the hours spent scrolling through social media, the compulsive need to stay constantly updated – and questioning their impact on our lives. Are these habits adding value, or are they a source of stress and distraction? Are we controlling our devices, or are they controlling us?

Once we clearly understand our current digital habits, the next step is learning how to change them. This isn't about drastic measures like completely giving up smartphones or abandoning social media; it's about learning to use these tools in a way that aligns with our values and real-life priorities. It's about finding a balance that allows us to reap the benefits of technology without letting it overshadow other important aspects of our lives.

One of the key themes of this chapter is setting intentions for technology use. This means consciously deciding why and how to use each digital tool. It's about using technology with a purpose – whether it's for work, education, or meaningful social connections – rather than out of habit or boredom. Intentionality is the cornerstone of mindful technology use, and it's a skill that, like any other, requires practice and dedication to develop.

Another important aspect of mindful technology use is learning how to disconnect. In today's always-on culture, disconnecting can feel uncomfortable, even anxiety-inducing. However, regularly stepping away from digital devices is essential for mental health and well-being. This chapter offers practical advice on how to create spaces and times free from digital interference, allowing our minds to rest and recharge.

Mindful technology use also extends to how we communicate online. Digital communication, while convenient, often lacks the nuances and emotional depth of face-to-face interactions. This section of the chapter explores how to communicate more thoughtfully and effectively in the digital world, ensuring that our online interactions are respectful, meaningful, and add positively to our lives and the lives of others.

Furthermore, this chapter addresses the challenge of dealing with digital overload – the constant barrage of information and stimuli that can lead to feelings of overwhelm and stress. Learning how to curate our digital consumption, set boundaries, and prioritize our digital tasks is essential for maintaining a healthy relationship with technology.

Ultimately, cultivating mindful technology use is a continuous journey, not a one-time fix. It's about regularly reassessing our habits, staying open to change, and being mindful of the evolving role of technology in our lives. This chapter aims to provide readers with the tools and insights they need to embark on this journey, helping them use technology in an enriching, intentional, and harmonious way with their overall well-being.

Understanding Mindful Technology Use

In the digitally saturated landscape of the 21st century, the concept of 'mindful technology use' has emerged as a crucial aspect of maintaining a healthy digital life. This section defines mindful technology use and explores the distinction between automatic, chronic use of technology and a more intentional, conscious approach.

Defining Mindful Technology Use

Mindful technology use is essentially about being present and intentional with how we interact with digital devices. It's a conscious approach to technology, where every swipe, click, or scroll is a deliberate choice, not just an automatic response to a notification or a habitual time-filler. This mindful approach helps us stay aligned with our real-life priorities and values, ensuring that our digital interactions serve us, not the other way around.

Mindfulness, in general, is the quality of being fully present and engaged at the moment, aware of our thoughts and actions, and not overly reactive or overwhelmed by external things. When applied to technology use, it means knowing why we use technology, how it makes us feel, and whether it benefits our lives.

Automatic vs. Intentional Use of Technology

The automatic, chronic use of technology is often characterized by mindless scrolling, compulsive checking of notifications, and using digital devices as a default activity to fill every spare moment. This type of usage is typically unreflective and reactive. It's driven more by habit or a desire to escape boredom or uncomfortable feelings than by a conscious decision. Over time, this can lead to a disconnection from real life, where we miss out on face-to-face interactions, real-world experiences, and even our own internal thoughts and emotions.

In contrast, intentional technology use is about making conscious choices. It involves pausing before picking up your phone and asking yourself why you're doing it. Are you checking your email because you expect an important message, or are you just trying to kill time? Are you scrolling through social media because you're genuinely interested in what your friends are up to, or are you just trying to avoid feeling lonely?

Intentional use also means setting boundaries around technology to ensure it doesn't interfere with important aspects of life, like relationships, work, and personal well-being. It's about using technology to enhance your life and connect meaningfully rather than letting it use you.

Benefits of Mindful Technology Use

Embracing a mindful approach to technology comes with numerous benefits. It can lead to improved mental health, as it helps prevent feelings of overwhelm and anxiety that often accompany excessive digital consumption. It can enhance relationships as you become more present and engaged with the people around you. It can also boost productivity and creativity by allowing you to disconnect, reflect, and engage in other activities that fuel your creativity.

Practicing Mindful Technology Use

To practice mindful technology use, become more aware of your digital habits. Notice when you reach for your phone and what triggers this action. Is it boredom, habit, or a specific need? Next, begin setting intentions for your technology use. Decide what you want to accomplish with your time online before you log on. And finally, create digital-free spaces and times in your day to disconnect and engage in other activities.

Self-Assessment and Reflection

Embarking on a journey towards mindful technology use necessitates a thorough self-assessment and reflection on our current habits. This reflective process helps us uncover the nature of our relationship with digital devices, laying the groundwork for meaningful change.

Starting the Self-Assessment

The first step in self-assessment is observation. Before modifying your habits, spend a few days observing your technology usage. Note the moments you reach for your phone, the duration of your usage, and the activities you engage in. This observation period is not about judgment or immediate change but about awareness.

Reflective Questions for Deeper Insights

As you observe your digital habits, ponder over these reflective questions to gain a deeper understanding of your technology use:

1. **What Triggers My Technology Use?** Consider what prompts you to use technology. Is it boredom, loneliness, anxiety, or the need to feel connected? Understanding your triggers can reveal underlying emotions or patterns driving your digital behavior.

2. **How Do I Feel Before, During, and After Using Technology?** Assess your emotional state at these three stages. Do you feel anxious before using it and relieved after, or is it the other way around? Your emotions can indicate whether technology is a source of comfort or stress.

3. **What Is My Most Frequently Used App or Service, and Why?** Identifying the apps or services you use most can illuminate what you seek from your digital interactions. Is it

information, entertainment, social connection, or something else?

4. **When Am I Most Likely to Use Technology Excessively?** Look for patterns in your usage. Are there specific times of day, situations, or feelings that lead to prolonged use? Recognizing these patterns is crucial in managing them.

5. **What Activities Am I Neglecting Due to Technology Use?** Reflect on what aspects of your life are impacted by excessive technology use. Are you spending less time on hobbies, with family, or engaging in physical activity?

6. **Does My Technology Use Align With My Values and Goals?** Consider whether your digital habits harmonise with your values and life goals. Does your technology use support or hinder your aspirations?

7. **How Do I Want Technology to Fit into My Life?** Envision your ideal relationship with technology. What does balanced use look like for you, and what role do you want digital devices to play in your daily life?

Documenting Your Reflections

Writing down your observations and responses to these questions can be incredibly insightful. It creates a tangible record of your current habits and thought processes, serving as a baseline for measuring future progress.

Analyzing Patterns and Making Connections

After a period of observation and reflection, look for patterns in your responses. These patterns can reveal a lot about your relationship with technology. Are specific emotional or situational triggers consistently leading to increased screen time? Are certain apps or activities disproportionately dominating your time?

Setting the Stage for Change

This self-assessment and reflection process is the first step towards mindful technology use. It sets the stage for informed and intentional changes. You're better equipped to make meaningful adjustments in your digital life with a clear understanding of your current habits and underlying drivers.

Embracing Self-Discovery

Finally, approach this self-assessment as an opportunity for self-discovery and growth. Understanding your technology habits is not just about reducing screen time; it's about gaining insights into your behaviors, motivations, and needs. This understanding is invaluable as you strive for a more balanced and fulfilling digital life.

Mindfulness Exercises for Digital Use

Integrating mindfulness exercises into our digital routines can be transformative in pursuing mindful technology use. Mindfulness, the practice of being fully present and engaged in the moment, can help mitigate the compulsive patterns of digital consumption. By incorporating simple yet effective mindfulness techniques, we can cultivate a more intentional and controlled relationship with our devices. This article explores practical mindfulness exercises that can be applied to technology use, enhancing our awareness and control over our digital habits.

One of the most straightforward yet powerful mindfulness exercises is to pause before checking your devices. This pause is a moment of self-awareness, where you ask yourself why you are reaching for the device. Is it out of habit or boredom, or is there a specific purpose? This brief moment of introspection can help you make a conscious decision about whether or not to use the device.

Another effective technique is to practice conscious breathing before opening apps, especially those you find absorbing or time-consuming, like social media or news feeds. Before you tap on the app, take a few deep breaths. This practice centres your mind and prepares you for a more controlled and aware engagement with the app. It acts as a mental buffer between the compulsion to use the app and the action of using it.

Setting intentions is a critical component of mindfulness, and it can be especially beneficial when applied to technology use. Before beginning any digital task, whether responding to emails, working on a digital project, or even engaging in leisure activities like gaming or browsing, take a moment to articulate your intention. What do you hope to achieve? How long do you intend to engage in this activity? Setting clear intentions can help keep your technology use purposeful and on track.

Adjust your notification settings to reduce unnecessary interruptions, and practice mindfulness when you do receive notifications. When your device pings, take a moment to notice your impulse to check the notification immediately. Acknowledge this impulse and then decide mindfully whether or not this notification requires your immediate attention.

You can use certain apps or features on your device as 'mindfulness bells' reminders to bring your attention back to the present moment. For example, every time you unlock your phone, let that action remind you to take a breath and be aware of your surroundings and state of mind.

Use your device to log moments of gratitude throughout your day. This can be done through a digital journal or note-taking app. This practice brings mindfulness into your digital life and fosters a positive mindset.

Be mindful of the content you consume. Before browsing or scrolling, remember to be selective and intentional about what you read, watch, or listen to. Ask yourself whether this content is beneficial, uplifting, or necessary.

Periodically throughout the day, check in with yourself to assess your state of mind and your technology use. Are you feeling anxious, distracted, or overwhelmed? These check-ins can be opportunities to reset and make mindful choices about continuing or ceasing your digital activity.

Incorporating mindfulness exercises into our digital routines offers a pathway to more conscious and intentional technology use. By pausing before engaging, setting intentions, and being fully present in our digital interactions, we can mitigate the compulsive and often mindless patterns of device usage. Mindfulness brings balance to our digital lives, ensuring that our technology use is aligned with our broader life goals and well-being.

Mindful Communication Online

Mindful communication in the digital realm is a critical aspect of our interactions today. With most of our conversations occurring online via social media, emails, and messaging platforms, how we express ourselves digitally has profound implications on our relationships and our personal and professional reputations. This article delves into how to navigate the digital space with mindfulness, ensuring that our communication is respectful, thoughtful, and aware of the lasting impact it can have.

Mindful communication online starts with the awareness that digital words are permanent. Unlike spoken words, what we write and share online can remain indefinitely, accessible to a broad audience, and open to interpretation. This permanence necessitates a thoughtful approach to posting, sharing, or emailing.

In the fast-paced online world, there's often pressure to respond quickly. However, mindful communication involves taking a moment to reflect before replying. It's about considering your response's tone, content, and implications. Ask yourself if your reply adds value to the conversation and if it reflects your true intentions.

Understanding that tone can easily be misconstrued in digital communication is crucial. Without the benefit of vocal inflexions, pauses, and body language, written words can sometimes convey a different meaning or emotion. Being explicit about your feelings and asking clarifying questions when in doubt can prevent misunderstandings.

Empathy – the ability to understand and share the feelings of another – is key in mindful online communication. It involves reading between the lines and being sensitive to what the other person might be feeling or going through. This understanding can guide the way you frame your responses, making them more compassionate and considerate.

Be mindful of privacy and consent, especially when sharing information or images that involve others. Always ask for permission before posting photos or sensitive information about someone else. This respect for privacy extends to being cautious about over-sharing personal details about your life.

Every digital interaction contributes to your digital footprint. Be conscious of the image you are creating through your online communications. This awareness is especially crucial in professional contexts, where digital interactions can impact your career and professional relationships.

Avoid impulsive posts or messages, especially when emotional. If you're feeling angry, upset, or overly excited, it might be wise to step away from the keyboard and revisit the message later with a clearer mind.

Aim to practice kindness in all your online interactions. This doesn't mean you can't engage in debates or express your opinion, but it does mean doing so respectfully and constructively. Avoiding online confrontations and spreading positive messages can promote a healthier online environment.

Remember that digital communication is just one aspect of your relationships. Where possible, balance online interactions with face-to-face or voice conversations. This balance can lead to deeper and more meaningful relationships.

Mindful communication online is not just about what we say but also how and why we say it. It's about being intentional, respectful, and empathetic in digital interactions. By practising these principles, we contribute to a positive digital environment and ensure that our online presence aligns with our real-world values and identity.

Dealing with Digital Overload

Dealing with digital overload is increasingly becoming necessary in our information-saturated age. Every day, we are bombarded with constant emails, social media updates, news articles, and notifications. This relentless flow can lead to information overload, overwhelming us, stress, and less productivity. Managing this deluge effectively is essential for maintaining mental clarity and focus. Here, we discuss strategies to curate digital content and limit the overwhelming influx of information.

Curating Your Digital Content

1. **Selective Engagement**: Be selective about the content you engage with online. Prioritize quality over quantity and choose sources that add value and relevance to your life. This might mean following fewer but more meaningful social media accounts or subscribing to a limited number of comprehensive news channels.

2. **Use Content Aggregators**: Utilize content aggregators or RSS feeds that consolidate content from various sources into one platform. This allows you to access diverse content in a single location, reducing the need to visit multiple websites or apps.

3. **Customize News Feeds and Notifications**: Customize your news feeds and notifications to align with your interests and current needs. Many social media platforms and news apps allow you to tailor the content you receive, helping you stay focused on what's important.

Managing Email Overload

1. **Regular Unsubscribing**: Regularly unsubscribe from newsletters or email lists that no longer serve your interests or needs. This simple action can significantly reduce the volume of emails you receive daily.

2. **Email Filters and Folders**: Utilize email filters and folders to organize your inbox. Filters can automatically sort emails into specific folders, making managing and prioritising your responses easier.

3. **Designated Times for Email Checking**: Instead of constantly checking your email throughout the day, designate specific times for this task. This approach reduces the distraction caused by frequent email notifications and increases productivity.

Limiting Information Flow

1. **Digital Tools for Limiting Access**: Use digital tools like website blockers to limit your access to particularly distracting or time-consuming websites during work hours or designated focus times.

2. **Setting Time Limits**: Set time limits for browsing or using social media. Most smartphones now come with screen time management features that allow you to set daily limits for specific apps.

3. **Scheduled Digital Detoxes**: Implement regular digital detoxes – periods where you step away from all digital devices. This could be certain hours of the day, weekends, or specific holidays.

Mindful Consumption

1. **Practicing Mindfulness**: Practice mindfulness when engaging with digital content. Ask yourself whether the content you consume is beneficial, and be aware of how it impacts your emotions and thoughts.

2. **Quality over Quantity**: Focus on consuming enriching content that aligns with your personal and professional goals. Quality content should leave you feeling informed, inspired, or educated, rather than drained or overwhelmed.

3. Effectively managing digital overload requires a combination of practical strategies and mindful practices. By curating digital content, managing emails efficiently, limiting the flow of information, and engaging with content mindfully, we can significantly reduce the stress and anxiety associated with digital overload. These practices help declutter our digital lives, reclaim our focus, and enhance our overall digital well-being.

Maintaining mindful technology practices

Maintaining mindful technology practices over the long term and incorporating them into family and work life are essential to creating a balanced relationship with digital devices. As technology continues evolving and integrating more into our daily routines, staying vigilant about our digital habits becomes increasingly essential. This article delves into strategies for sustaining mindful technology practices in the long term and integrating these practices into family and workplace dynamics.

Long-Term Mindful Technology Practices

The digital landscape is ever-changing, with new apps, platforms, and devices constantly emerging. As such, our approach to technology needs to be dynamic and adaptable. Regularly reassessing our digital habits is crucial – what worked a few months ago might not be effective now. This reassessment involves reflecting on our current technology use, identifying areas for improvement, and adjusting our strategies accordingly. For instance, if you find yourself slipping back into old habits of checking your phone first thing in the morning, it might be time to revisit and strengthen your digital routines.

Awareness of evolving technology trends and their potential impact on our lives can help us make informed decisions about our digital consumption. This means staying updated about the latest apps and devices and comprehending their functionalities and implications. For example, understanding how specific social media algorithms work can inform our decisions about how and when to use these platforms.

Long-term mindful technology use also involves setting and maintaining personal boundaries. This might include specific no-tech times during the day, tech-free zones in the home, or personal rules about not using technology during meals or family time. Consistently adhering to these boundaries can help solidify them as habits.

Cultivating interests and hobbies that don't involve screens is another effective strategy for maintaining long-term mindful technology use. Whether outdoor activities, reading, cooking, or arts and crafts, these hobbies can provide a fulfilling and necessary counterbalance to our digital lives.

Incorporating Mindfulness into Family and Work Life

Creating a family culture that values mindful technology use begins with setting a good example. Parents and caregivers can lead by example by adhering to their mindful technology practices. Additionally, involving the entire family in setting technology guidelines can encourage buy-in and cooperation. This could include family discussions about screen time, negotiating tech-free times, and planning family activities that don't involve screens.

One practical approach is establishing tech-free zones or times in the home, such as during meals, an hour before bedtime, or weekend mornings. Encouraging open conversations about how technology affects everyone's well-being can also be beneficial. For example, discussing how excessive screen time can impact sleep or how specific online interactions make family members feel.

Fostering a culture of mindful technology use in the workplace can boost productivity and improve employee well-being. Employers and team leaders can set the tone by encouraging breaks from screens, establishing 'email-free' times during the day, and promoting face-to-face meetings when possible.

Creating team agreements on how to use technology can also be effective. For instance, teams might agree not to send work emails outside business hours or to use specific communication channels for different messages. Encouraging employees to take regular breaks away from their screens and providing spaces for relaxation and offline interaction can also promote a more mindful approach to technology.

Additionally, offering training or resources on digital wellness can empower employees to make informed choices about their technology use. This could include workshops on digital mindfulness, information about the impact of screen time on health, or tips on managing digital distractions.

Maintaining mindful technology practices over the long term and integrating these practices into family and work life is vital for navigating the digital world healthily and sustainably. We can sustain a balanced digital life by continually reassessing our habits, staying informed about technology trends, setting personal boundaries, and embracing tech-free activities. Similarly, encouraging mindful technology use among family members and within the workplace can create supportive environments that foster digital well-being. As we become more conscious of our digital interactions and their impact, we can enjoy the benefits of technology without letting it dominate our lives.

6

Strengthening Real-World Connections

"Strengthening Real-World Connections" opens the door to a critical conversation about the significance of nurturing offline relationships in our increasingly digital world. As we dive into this chapter, we explore the profound value and inherent necessity of fostering solid and meaningful connections outside the realm of screens and digital interfaces. This chapter is not just an analysis or a set of recommendations; it is a call to action, a reminder of the fundamental human need for genuine, face-to-face interaction and the rich, fulfilling relationships it cultivates.

In an era where digital devices often mediate our social interactions, the importance of direct, in-person connections can sometimes be overshadowed. The ease and convenience of digital communication have revolutionized the way we interact, enabling us to stay connected across vast distances. However, this digital convenience comes with a caveat – the potential dilution of the depth and quality of our relationships. This chapter delves into the unique qualities of offline relationships – the depth of conversation, the nuances of body language and tone, and the emotional richness that can only be fully experienced in the physical presence of others.

The first aspect we explore is the psychology of face-to-face interaction. There's a certain magic in sharing a space with someone, in observing their expressions and reactions, in physically experiencing the give-and-take of a conversation. Such interactions engage our emotions and senses in ways that digital communication cannot replicate. We'll look at how these interactions not only enhance our relationships but also contribute to our emotional and psychological well-being.

Then, we turn our focus to family – often our most significant and enduring relationships. In the digital age, family time can sometimes become secondary to our online engagements. This chapter discusses reclaiming this precious time offering practical strategies for creating tech-free family environments. We delve into activities that foster familial bonding, emphasizing creating shared experiences free from digital distractions.

Community involvement and social responsibility form another cornerstone of this chapter. Involvement in community activities and volunteer work isn't just about giving back; it's about connecting with others, understanding diverse perspectives, and building a sense of belonging. We discuss the multifaceted benefits of community engagement – from the personal satisfaction and growth it fosters to the positive societal impact it generates.

Building and maintaining friendships in the real world can sometimes feel more challenging in a digital age. This chapter provides insights into nurturing these crucial connections. It's about rediscovering the joy of spontaneous coffee dates, the excitement of group adventures, and the comfort of heartfelt conversations. We explore how these interactions enrich our lives, providing support, laughter, and a sense of connection that virtual interactions often lack.

Lastly, the chapter acknowledges the undeniable role that digital tools play in our lives and explores how to strike a balance between online and offline socialization. It's about using technology as a bridge to enhance real-world relationships, not as a barrier. We discuss transitioning from online interactions to deepening these connections in the physical world and how to navigate this delicate balance.

Throughout this chapter, the emphasis is on action – on taking deliberate steps to strengthen our real-world connections. In an age where we can quickly lose ourselves in the digital world, this chapter serves as a reminder of the irreplaceable value of personal, direct human connections. It encourages readers to step back from their screens, look up and around, and invest in relationships that truly enrich their lives. This exploration into strengthening real-world connections is more than a guide; it is a journey towards rediscovering the essence of human interaction in its most authentic form.

The Psychology of Face-to-Face Interaction

The integral role of face-to-face interaction in human relationships cannot be overstated, especially in an age where digital communication increasingly supplants in-person connections. Delving into the psychology of face-to-face interaction reveals why these engagements are vital to our emotional well-being and how they foster more profound understanding and stronger emotional bonds than digital interactions.

Face-to-face communication is the most natural and effective mode of human interaction. When we communicate in person, we engage verbally and through non-verbal cues such as body language, facial expressions, gestures, and tone of voice. These non-verbal elements add depth and richness to our conversations, allowing us to convey and interpret emotions and intentions with a level of nuance that is often absent in digital communication.

Body language and facial expressions often convey more than words alone can express. A warm smile, a reassuring touch, or an empathetic nod can communicate understanding and support without a single word. In contrast, a furrowed brow, crossed arms, or averted gaze can express displeasure, disagreement, or discomfort. These subtle cues are integral to understanding the emotional context of a conversation and responding appropriately.

The tone of voice carries emotional information that text on a screen cannot convey. Inflexions, volume, and pace of speech can express excitement, sarcasm, concern, or anger, providing an additional layer of context to the spoken word. This auditory information helps us decode the true meaning behind the words, often revealing emotions that might be concealed or misunderstood in written communication.

The benefits of in-person communication extend far beyond the conveyance of information. They touch on several aspects of our psychological well-being.

Face-to-face interactions foster a deeper emotional connection between individuals. Seeing and interpreting each other's emotions in real time enhances empathy and understanding. This connection is critical in building and maintaining solid relationships with family, friends, or colleagues. Empathy, facilitated by direct interaction, strengthens social bonds and fosters a sense of belonging and community.

Trust is more easily established and reinforced in face-to-face interactions. Physical presence, eye contact, and active listening are fundamental in building rapport and creating and maintaining trust. Trust developed through direct interactions lays the foundation for solid and lasting relationships in personal and professional settings.

Managing conflicts is often more effective in person. The complexity of emotions and conflict misunderstandings can be challenging to navigate through digital channels. Face-to-face communication allows for immediate feedback, clarification, and the opportunity to employ empathy and understanding, which are crucial for resolution.

Research suggests that we are more likely to remember information and interactions that occur in person. The multisensory experience of a face-to-face conversation involving visual, auditory, and sometimes tactile stimuli creates a more memorable and impactful experience than a digital exchange.

Direct social interactions are linked to better mental health. Conversations with others can reduce feelings of anxiety and depression and boost self-esteem and life satisfaction. The support and connection during in-person interactions contribute significantly to our psychological resilience.

While digital communication is invaluable for bridging distances and providing convenient ways to stay connected, it has limitations. Online interactions often lack the emotional depth and subtleties provided by non-verbal cues. Misunderstandings are common, and the emotional connection can feel less intense or genuine. Additionally, overusing digital communication can lead to feelings of isolation and loneliness despite being constantly connected.

Recognizing the value of face-to-face interaction prompts a reevaluation of our communication choices. It involves making a conscious effort to seek out and prioritize in-person meetings and conversations. It's about finding a balance, where digital tools are used to facilitate, not replace, the rich, multifaceted experience of direct human interaction.

In a world where digital communication is often the default, actively seeking out face-to-face interactions is both a challenge and a necessity. It requires us to step away from our screens and engage with the world and the people around us in a more meaningful, connected way. This approach not only enriches our relationships but also enhances our overall psychological well-being.

In conclusion, the psychological benefits of face-to-face interaction are profound and multifaceted. As we navigate our digitally connected lives, it's essential to remember the irreplaceable value of in-person communication in fostering understanding, empathy, and deep emotional connections. By making a conscious effort to engage more in face-to-face interactions, we can strengthen our relationships and enrich our emotional and psychological health.

Reclaiming Family Time

Reclaiming family time from the clutches of digital distractions has become increasingly important in the age of constant connectivity. The digital era, while bringing us closer to the world at large, often distances us from those closest to us – our family. This article explores strategies to make family time more engaging and fulfilling, free from the interference of digital devices. It highlights the importance of tech-free family activities and creating tech-free zones in the home, offering a pathway to deeper familial connections and more meaningful interactions.

Understanding the Impact of Digital Devices on Family Dynamics

Before delving into the strategies, it's crucial to understand how pervasive digital device usage can affect family dynamics. Constant attention to screens can lead to missed opportunities for bonding, communication breakdowns, and a general sense of disconnection within the family unit. Recognizing these impacts is the first step towards making a positive change.

Establishing Tech-Free Zones and Times

One of the most effective ways to reclaim family time is by establishing tech-free zones and times within the household. This could mean no phones at the dinner table, no TV during mealtimes, or setting aside certain evening hours as device-free. These simple rules help create an environment where family members can interact without digital interruptions, fostering closer relationships and better communication.

Engaging in Tech-Free Family Activities

Shared meals are not just about eating; they are opportunities for conversation, sharing experiences, and enjoying each other's company. Encouraging open dialogue, storytelling, or even playing conversation-starter games can make mealtime a key event for family bonding.

Outdoor activities like hiking, biking, picnics, or a simple walk in the park provide a refreshing break from technology. These adventures offer physical exercise and the chance to explore and appreciate nature together, creating lasting memories.

Organizing a family board game night is a fantastic way to engage in playful and competitive activities. Board games cater to all ages and often encourage strategic thinking, teamwork, and fun.

Participating in creative activities such as arts and crafts, cooking or baking together, or even engaging in DIY home projects can be educational and enjoyable. These activities allow family members to express their creativity, learn new skills, and work together towards a common goal.

Setting aside time for reading books, telling stories, or listening to audiobooks can be relaxing and intellectually stimulating. This can be particularly beneficial for young children, as it fosters a love for reading and enhances their listening and comprehension skills.

Encouraging Open Communication About Technology Use

Openly discussing the role of technology in your family's life is vital. Conversations about how each family member feels about technology and its impact on their relationships can lead to a mutual understanding and more mindful usage. These discussions also allow children to voice their opinions and learn about the responsible use of technology.

Leading by Example

For parents, leading by example is crucial. Demonstrating balanced technology use and actively participating in tech-free activities sets a positive precedent for the rest of the family. Children who see their parents prioritizing family time over screens are more likely to follow suit.

Balancing Online and Offline Activities

While tech-free time is necessary, it's also essential to recognize that technology can be a tool for family bonding when used appropriately. This could include watching a movie together, playing video games, or engaging in educational online activities. The key is to balance these digital activities with offline interactions.

Regularly Revisiting and Adjusting Family Tech Policies

As technology evolves and children grow, family tech policies may need revisited and adjusted. Regular family meetings to discuss these policies can ensure they remain relevant and practical. These meetings can also serve as a platform for family members to share new ideas for tech-free activities.

Reclaiming family time in the digital age is about balancing the online and offline worlds. It's about recognizing the value of presence, communication, and shared experiences. By establishing tech-free zones and times, engaging in various tech-free activities, and fostering open communication about technology use, families can strengthen their bonds and enjoy more prosperous, more fulfilling relationships. In doing so, we not only enhance our familial connections but also model healthy digital habits for future generations.

Community Engagement and Social Responsibility

Community engagement and social responsibility play pivotal roles in enriching our lives and our societies. Participation in local events, community projects, or volunteer work offers numerous benefits, ranging from enhanced personal growth to the betterment of society. This discussion focuses on how involvement in these activities fosters a sense of belonging, contributes to personal development, and underpins societal well-being.

Enhancing a Sense of Belonging Through Community Engagement

Engaging in community activities provides a profound sense of belonging and connection. In a world where individualism often takes precedence, community involvement brings people together for a common purpose. Participating in local events, be it a neighbourhood clean-up, a cultural festival, or a public meeting, allows individuals to connect with their neighbours and local leaders. These interactions foster a sense of belonging and a stronger connection to one's local environment. They break down barriers, build bridges across diverse groups, and cultivate a spirit of unity and solidarity.

Personal Growth and Development

Community engagement is also a powerful catalyst for personal growth. It offers opportunities to develop new skills, gain diverse perspectives, and enhance one's understanding of societal issues. Volunteering, for instance, can challenge individuals to step out of their comfort zones, leading to increased self-confidence and resilience. It can also provide valuable experiences that aid in career development, such as leadership, teamwork, and problem-solving skills.

Moreover, community involvement often increases awareness and empathy towards social issues. It allows individuals to witness firsthand the challenges others face in their communities, fostering a deeper understanding and compassion. This empathy motivates a more informed and conscientious approach to social responsibility.

Contribution to Societal Well-Being

The impact of community engagement extends far beyond individual benefits. It plays a crucial role in societal well-being. When citizens actively participate in community activities and volunteer work, they contribute to the social capital of their area. They help build stronger, more cohesive communities better equipped to face challenges and support their members.

Community projects and volunteer work can address various societal needs – from environmental conservation and education to supporting the underprivileged and enhancing public safety. These efforts collectively contribute to the development and improvement of society. They also serve as examples of proactive citizenship, inspiring others to take action and engage in their communities.

Building Networks and Relationships

Community engagement is also about building networks and relationships supporting personal and communal goals. These networks are invaluable resources for sharing knowledge, skills, and support. They create channels through which individuals and groups can mobilize for various causes, advocate for change, and assist those in need.

Encouraging Inclusivity and Diversity

Participating in community activities promotes inclusivity and diversity. It allows individuals from different backgrounds, cultures, and age groups to come together and collaborate. This diversity enriches community projects, bringing in various perspectives and ideas that can lead to more innovative and practical solutions to communal challenges.

Long-Term Impact and Legacy

Lastly, the long-term impact of active community involvement cannot be understated. It creates a legacy of service, compassion, and civic responsibility. This legacy benefits current community members and sets a positive example for future generations, teaching them the value of service, cooperation, and social responsibility.

Community engagement and social responsibility involvement is a fulfilling journey that enriches both the individual and society. It nurtures a sense of belonging, fosters personal growth, and contributes significantly to societal well-being. Individuals can actively shape more vibrant, resilient, and compassionate communities by participating in local events, community projects, and volunteer work. This engagement is not just a contribution to society but an investment in the collective future of our communities and the broader world.

Building and Maintaining Friendships Offline

Building and maintaining friendships offline holds special significance in an era where digital interactions often overshadow personal connections. Nurturing these relationships through in-person interactions brings a depth and richness that virtual connections often lack. This discussion delves into the value of face-to-face friendships and explores various ways to initiate and sustain these meaningful bonds.

The Value of Offline Friendships

Offline friendships provide emotional and psychological depth that is hard to replicate digitally. In-person interactions allow us to perceive and respond to the subtle nuances of body language, tone of voice, and facial expressions, fostering a deeper understanding and empathy. These interactions are vital for building solid and lasting friendships that contribute significantly to our emotional well-being and happiness.

Initiating Offline Friendships

1. **Interest-Based Clubs or Groups**: Joining clubs or groups based on personal interests or hobbies is an excellent way to meet like-minded individuals. Whether it's a book club, a hiking group, a cooking class, or a photography club, these settings offer a natural platform for initiating conversations and forming connections.

2. **Community Events and Volunteering**: Participating in community events, social gatherings, or volunteer activities can also provide opportunities to meet new people. These activities often foster a sense of teamwork and camaraderie, which are conducive to forming friendships.

3. **Sports and Fitness Activities**: Engaging in team sports, fitness classes, or outdoor activities can be another avenue to connect with others. Shared physical activities promote health and well-being and create an environment for easy socialization.

4. **Workshops and Educational Courses**: Attending workshops, seminars, or courses offers the dual benefit of learning a new skill and meeting people with similar interests. These settings often encourage group interaction and discussions, facilitating the building of new friendships.

Sustaining Offline Friendships

1. **Regular Meet-ups**: Once friendships are formed, it's important to nurture them through regular meet-ups. Setting up routine coffee dates, meals, movie nights, or walks can help maintain and strengthen these relationships.

2. **Shared Experiences**: Creating shared experiences is key to deepening friendships. This could involve traveling together, attending concerts or events, or undertaking a shared project or challenge.

3. **Open and Honest Communication**: Like any relationship, friendships thrive on open and honest communication. Face-to-face conversations allow for more sincere communication, essential for a strong bond.

4. **Support and Encouragement**: Being there for friends during tough times, celebrating their successes, and offering support and encouragement are crucial to sustaining friendships. These actions reinforce the trust and dependability foundational to any close relationship.

5. **Balancing Digital and In-Person Interactions**: While in-person interactions are key, it's also practical to use digital tools to stay connected, especially when in-person meetings are impossible. The goal is to find a balance where digital interactions complement rather than replace face-to-face connections.

Building and maintaining offline friendships in today's digital world is both a challenge and an opportunity. These relationships bring immeasurable value to our lives, providing support, joy, and a sense of belonging. By actively seeking out and nurturing these connections through regular in-person interactions and shared experiences, we can foster a network of meaningful friendships that enrich our lives in ways that digital connections cannot.

Balancing Digital and Real-World Socialization

In today's interconnected world, where digital and real-world socialization coexist, striking a balance has become more crucial. While digital tools have revolutionized how we connect, communicate, and maintain relationships, they should complement, not replace, the richness of in-person interactions. This discussion focuses on acknowledging the role of digital tools in facilitating connections, emphasizing the importance of balancing these with real-world interactions, and navigating the transition from online to offline relationships.

The Complementary Role of Digital Tools

Digital tools have undeniably made staying connected with friends, family, and colleagues easier across distances. Social media, messaging apps, and video calls have broken geographical barriers, allowing continuous communication and interaction. They are handy for maintaining long-distance relationships offering a platform for sharing life updates, memorable moments, and everyday happenings.

However, these digital interactions are often surface-level and lack the depth that face-to-face interactions provide. The key is to use these tools as a complement to, rather than a substitute for, real-world socialization. They should be seen as a means to stay connected when physical presence isn't possible, not as the default mode of building and maintaining relationships.

Enhancing In-Person Relationships Through Technology

Technology, when used mindfully, can enhance in-person relationships. It can be a tool for planning and coordinating meetups, sharing interests, or continuing conversations that began online. For instance, friends can use social media to share and discuss topics of mutual interest, leading to deeper discussions during in-person meetups.

Moreover, digital tools can bridge the transition from online to offline interactions. Many relationships today begin online through social media, dating apps, or online forums. Technology can facilitate the initial connection and communication, setting the stage for face-to-face meetings. However, transitioning to offline interaction is crucial for the relationship to evolve and deepen.

Navigating the Transition from Online to Offline Interactions

The transition from online to offline interactions can be challenging but is integral to forming more profound connections. Here are some strategies to navigate this transition:

1. **Initiate Face-to-Face Meetings**: When a relationship formed online reaches a certain level of comfort and trust,

initiate a plan to meet in person. This could be a casual meetup in a public place, a coffee date, or an activity you enjoy.

2. **Set Realistic Expectations**: Understand that people may present themselves differently online than in person. Approach the first offline meeting with openness and without overly rigid expectations.

3. **Use Online Interactions as a Foundation**: Leverage the knowledge and interests shared online as a foundation for offline interactions. This can provide a comfortable starting point for in-person conversations.

4. **Keep Safety in Mind**: When transitioning from an online to an offline relationship, especially with someone you've met online, prioritize safety. Meet in public places and consider informing a friend or family member about your plans.

Maintaining a Balance

Balancing digital and real-world socialization requires conscious effort. It involves:

- Making time for face-to-face interactions in your schedule.

- Being present during in-person meetings without the distraction of digital devices.

- Using digital communication to enhance and facilitate, but not replace, the richness of direct, personal interactions.

While digital tools play a significant role in today's social landscape, they are best used as adjuncts to enhance real-world relationships. Balancing online and offline interactions is crucial in developing and maintaining deeper, more meaningful relationships. By consciously navigating the transition from online to offline and understanding the unique value of face-to-face interactions, we can foster a well-rounded social life enriched by both digital and real-world connections.

-82-

＃ 7

Fostering Discipline in a Distracted World

This chapter opens a crucial dialogue about cultivating self-discipline amidst the relentless digital distractions that permeate our modern lives. In an era where our attention is constantly besieged by a barrage of notifications, social media feeds, and the ever-present allure of the internet, developing and maintaining focus and discipline has become a formidable challenge. This chapter aims to unravel the intricacies of self-discipline in the digital age, offering insights and strategies to navigate and triumph over the digital distractions that often divert us from our goals and aspirations.

The proliferation of digital technology, while offering unprecedented access to information and connectivity, has also ushered in an age of distraction. Every ping of a notification and every buzz of a smartphone compete for our attention, fragmenting our focus and diluting our concentration. In this digital landscape, the ability to maintain discipline and focus is not just an asset; it is a necessity. This chapter delves into understanding the nature of these digital temptations and distractions, uncovering why they are so compelling and how they can quickly derail our focus, productivity, and mental well-being.

Understanding digital temptations requires an exploration of the psychological mechanisms that drive them. We will examine the concept of instant gratification – the human tendency to favor immediate rewards over future benefits – which digital platforms expertly exploit. From the dopamine-driven feedback loops of social media to the endless scroll of news feeds, we will uncover the inner workings of these distractions and why our brains are wired to succumb to them. This knowledge is crucial in developing strategies to counteract these distractions, enabling us to make more informed, conscious decisions about our digital consumption.

However, understanding is only the first step. The crux of this chapter lies in offering practical, actionable strategies to enhance focus and minimize distractions. This includes a deep dive into techniques and tools to bolster concentration and productivity. Techniques like the Pomodoro Technique, which involves breaking work into intervals with short breaks, and time-blocking, where specific time slots are dedicated to specific tasks, can be transformative. We will also explore how technology can be harnessed to aid focus, from apps that block distracting websites to tools that help manage and prioritize tasks.

Creating an environment conducive to focus is also critical. This chapter section will guide readers in organizing a physical and digital space that fosters concentration and minimizes distractions. This includes setting up a clutter-free workspace, establishing clear boundaries for technology use, and understanding the importance of regular breaks to rejuvenate the mind.

Beyond the immediate environment and practical tools, this chapter emphasizes the significance of building and maintaining self-discipline routines. Self-discipline is not innate but a skill that can be developed and strengthened over time. We will discuss how to set clear, achievable goals, and how the power of routine and habit formation can be pivotal in fostering self-discipline. Building resilience against distractions is not just about willpower but about creating systems and routines supporting our larger objectives.

However, the path to self-discipline is not linear, and it is crucial to approach this journey with self-compassion and flexibility. The chapter will underscore the importance of recognizing that lapses are part of the learning process. It's not the occasional slip that defines our journey, but how we respond to it and what we learn from it. This section will guide maintaining discipline, dealing with setbacks, and adapting strategies to fit changing circumstances and goals.

As we navigate through this chapter, the overarching goal is to equip readers with a robust toolkit to manage the digital distractions that are inherent in today's world. It's about striking a balance — leveraging technology for its immense benefits while not letting it overpower our ability to focus and achieve our personal and professional goals.

"Fostering Discipline in a Distracted World" is more than a guide; it's a compass for navigating the digital landscape with intentionality and purpose. It aims to empower readers to take control of their digital interactions, cultivate a disciplined approach to their goals, and, ultimately, forge a path that leads to enhanced productivity, fulfilment, and well-being in a world where distractions are just a click away.

Understanding and Overcoming Digital Temptations

In a world increasingly dominated by digital devices and online platforms, understanding and overcoming digital temptations has become crucial to maintaining focus and productivity. The allure of the digital world is not accidental; it is intricately designed, tapping into the very workings of the human brain. To develop effective strategies against these temptations, we first must delve into why our brains are so susceptible to digital distractions and how these can derail our focus and productivity.

The Allure of Digital Distractions

Digital distractions, ranging from social media notifications to endless emails, are designed to capture and hold our attention. They often promise a quick, low-effort way to access entertainment, information, or social interaction. But why are they so alluring?

Instant Gratification

A significant factor is the concept of instant gratification. Humans naturally seek immediate rewards, a tendency rooted in our evolutionary history. In the past, quick responses to immediate opportunities or threats were crucial for survival. In the digital age, this translates into an inclination to prefer the immediate pleasure of a funny video or the instant response to a text message over long-term goals requiring sustained effort and not offering immediate rewards.

Dopamine-Driven Feedback Loops

Dopamine, a neurotransmitter associated with pleasure and reward, is central to understanding the allure of digital distractions. When we engage with digital platforms, mainly social media, we experience minor dopamine releases. Likes, comments, shares, and new content create a dopamine-driven feedback loop, reinforcing our actions and encouraging us to repeat them. This loop can lead to habitually checking devices and a constant craving for the rewards that digital interactions promise.

The Impact on Focus and Productivity

The impact of succumbing to these digital temptations is significant, especially regarding focus and productivity. While seemingly brief, each distraction can take a toll on our ability to concentrate. The brain takes time to refocus after each interruption, leading to what is known as the "attention residue" phenomenon. As a result, we work at a diminished capacity, struggling to regain our concentration level before the distraction.

Strategies to Resist and Overcome Digital Temptations

Overcoming digital temptations requires a multifaceted approach. By understanding the mechanics behind these distractions, we can employ strategies that tackle both the psychological pull and the chronic nature of our digital interactions.

Awareness and Mindfulness

The first step in combating digital distractions is awareness. Being mindful of your digital habits can help you recognize patterns of compulsive behavior. Mindfulness practices, such as reflecting before automatically reaching for your phone, can help interrupt these habitual responses.

Controlling the Digital Environment

Taking control of your digital environment is essential. This can include turning off non-essential notifications, setting specific times to check emails or social media, and using apps that limit your time on particular sites. By creating barriers to access, you reduce the likelihood of succumbing to digital temptations.

Establishing Routines and Boundaries

Establishing routines and boundaries around digital device usage can also be effective. This might involve designated periods of deep work without digital interruptions or tech-free times during the day, such as during meals or the first hour after waking up.

Replacing Digital Habits

Replacing digital habits with healthier alternatives can provide a dual benefit. Engaging in activities like reading, exercise, or hobbies can distract you from digital temptations and provide longer-term satisfaction and fulfillment.

Understanding the Triggers

Identifying the triggers that lead to digital distractions can help develop personalized strategies to combat them. For instance, if social media browsing is a way to avoid complex tasks, finding alternative coping mechanisms for stress can be helpful.

Understanding and overcoming digital temptations is a critical skill in today's world. By recognizing the psychological underpinnings of these distractions and employing strategic measures to counteract them, we can regain control over our attention and productivity. This journey is not about eliminating digital tools from our lives but about learning to use them in a way that is mindful, controlled, and aligned with our broader goals and well-being.

Ethan Ray

Strategies for Enhancing Focus and Minimizing Distractions

In an era where digital distractions are incessantly vying for our attention, the ability to focus has become a rare commodity. The barrage of notifications, the allure of social media, and the constant influx of emails can fragment our attention and significantly hamper our productivity. To combat this, we need to employ practical strategies that enhance focus and minimize distractions. This article explores various techniques, including the Pomodoro Technique, time-blocking, focus-enhancing tools and apps, and ways to create a conducive environment for concentration.

The Pomodoro Technique

Developed in the late 1980s by Francesco Cirillo, the Pomodoro Technique is a time management method that uses a timer to break work into intervals, traditionally 25 minutes in length, separated by short breaks. These intervals are known as "pomodoros", the plural in Italian for 'tomato', named after the tomato-shaped kitchen timer that Cirillo used as a university student.

The technique works on the principle of short, focused bursts of work followed by a break. This not only helps maintain high levels of concentration but also ensures regular rest periods, aiding mental agility. To implement the Pomodoro Technique, one needs to:

1. Choose a task to be accomplished.

2. Set the Pomodoro timer (typically for 25 minutes).

3. Work on the task until the timer rings.

4. Take a short break (5 minutes is the standard).

5. After four pomodoros, take a longer break (15-30 minutes).

This technique is particularly effective for large tasks or projects that can seem overwhelming. Breaking them down into manageable intervals can reduce anxiety and make the task seem more achievable.

Time-Blocking

Time-blocking is a method of time management that involves dedicating specific blocks of time to particular tasks or activities. This technique helps in organizing your day more efficiently and ensures that you allocate sufficient time to each task. Time-blocking can be particularly useful for tasks that require deep concentration, as it allows you to dedicate undisturbed time to these activities. It also helps in setting clear boundaries between work and leisure, which can be blurred in the digital age.

To effectively use time-blocking:

1. Start by identifying the tasks you need to accomplish.

2. Estimate how much time each task will require.

3. Block out time on your calendar for each task.

4. During each block, focus solely on the task at hand.

5. Avoid multitasking, as it can dilute your focus.

Focus-Enhancing Tools and Apps

In the digital age, various tools and apps can help enhance focus and minimize distractions. For instance, apps like Freedom, Cold Turkey, or StayFocusd allow users to block distracting websites and apps for specified periods. Other tools like Focus@Will provide music designed to enhance concentration.

Additionally, project management tools like Trello or Asana can help organize tasks and deadlines, making it easier to stay focused and on track.

Creating a Conducive Environment for Focus

The physical and digital environment plays a crucial role in our ability to focus. A clutter-free workspace can minimize distractions and aid concentration. Organizing your desk, having a comfortable chair, adequate lighting, and all necessary materials within reach can create an environment conducive to focus.

In terms of the digital environment, organizing your digital workspace is equally important. This involves decluttering your desktop, organizing files, and closing unnecessary tabs and applications. Using multiple desktops or screens for different types of work can also help maintain focus.

Setting Clear Boundaries for Technology Use

Setting clear boundaries for technology use is crucial in minimizing digital distractions. This might involve turning off notifications during work hours, setting specific times to check emails, or using your phone in Do Not Disturb mode while working on essential tasks.

The Role of Mindfulness and Meditation

Mindfulness and meditation are powerful tools for enhancing concentration. Mindfulness practices involve focusing on the present moment and observing your thoughts and sensations without judgment. This can help develop greater control over your attention, making it easier to focus when needed.

Meditation, particularly concentration meditation, can train your brain to focus better. Regular meditation has been shown to increase the grey matter in the brain, which is associated with attention, self-control, and sensory processing.

Implementing These Strategies

Implementing these strategies requires discipline and practice. It's about finding what works best for you and adapting these techniques to fit your work style and needs. Start by implementing one or two strategies and gradually incorporate more as you become comfortable.

The constant battle against digital distractions is ongoing, but with the right techniques and a conducive environment, enhancing focus and productivity is achievable. By employing methods like the Pomodoro Technique, time-blocking, using focus-enhancing tools, organizing your workspace, setting clear technology boundaries, and practising mindfulness and meditation, you can cultivate a deep and sustained concentration level. This boosts productivity and contributes to a more balanced and fulfilling professional and personal life.

Building and Maintaining Self-Discipline Routines

Self-discipline is a foundational pillar in the pursuit of personal and professional success. Yet, in a world teeming with digital distractions, maintaining this discipline can be a daunting challenge. Building and maintaining self-discipline routines are essential for staying focused on our goals despite the ever-present lure of notifications and online diversions. This article delves into strategies for establishing robust self-discipline routines, underscoring the importance of setting achievable goals, habit formation, resilience against distractions, and the often-overlooked necessity of self-compassion and flexibility in this journey.

The Power of Clear, Achievable Goals

The journey towards strong self-discipline begins with setting clear, achievable goals. Goals act as beacons, guiding our efforts and providing a sense of direction. When setting goals, it's essential to ensure they are specific, measurable, attainable, relevant, and time-bound (SMART). This framework helps in creating goals that are not only clear but also motivating and realistically achievable.

For instance, rather than setting a vague goal like "I want to be more productive," a SMART goal would be "I will dedicate two uninterrupted hours each morning to work on my project for the next month." This goal is specific (two uninterrupted hours), measurable (each morning), attainable (a realistic duration), relevant (focused on productivity), and time-bound (for the next month).

Establishing Routines and Habits

Once goals are set, the next step is establishing routines and habits that support these objectives. Routines provide structure and consistency, two critical elements in fostering self-discipline. By creating a daily routine, we automate our actions, making adhering to our plans easier and reducing the mental effort required to make daily decisions.

Habit formation is central to this process. Habits are actions we perform automatically and play a significant role in shaping our daily lives. Developing habits that align with our goals can significantly bolster our self-discipline. For instance, establishing a morning workout habit can be instrumental if your goal is to improve physical health. Initially, this requires conscious effort, but over time, it becomes an ingrained part of your routine.

Building Resilience Against Distractions

In an age where digital distractions are omnipresent, building resilience against these interruptions is vital. This involves creating strategies to minimize the impact of potential distractions and developing the mental fortitude to stay focused.

One effective strategy is the proactive management of your digital environment. This can include turning off unnecessary notifications, using apps that limit your time on social media, and setting aside specific times to check emails. Additionally, creating a physical workspace that minimizes distractions can significantly enhance your ability to maintain focus.

Mental resilience can be bolstered through mindfulness meditation, which enhances your ability to remain present and not succumb to fleeting distractions. It's also about recognizing and acknowledging the urge to engage in a distracting activity and consciously choosing to refocus on your task.

Embracing Self-Compassion and Flexibility

Self-compassion is an often overlooked yet crucial component of maintaining self-discipline. It's essential to recognize that building discipline is a process, and occasional lapses are inevitable. Being harsh on yourself for minor slip-ups can be counterproductive. Instead, approach these moments with understanding and kindness, learn from them, and use them as stepping stones towards your goal.

Flexibility is also crucial in maintaining discipline. Life is unpredictable, and rigid adherence to routines can sometimes be impractical. Flexibility means adjusting your patterns and habits as circumstances change while keeping your overall goals in sight. This adaptability prevents discouragement and helps in sustaining motivation over the long term.

Implementing Self-Discipline Routines

Implementing self-discipline routines requires patience and persistence. Start by integrating small changes into your daily life and gradually build upon them. Celebrate small victories along the way, as these reinforce your commitment to your goals and bolster your self-discipline.

It's also beneficial to periodically review and adjust your routines and goals. As you grow and evolve, so too will your objectives and the strategies you employ to achieve them. Regularly revisiting your goals ensures that your routines remain aligned with your aspirations.

Building and maintaining self-discipline in a distracted world is dynamic and ongoing. It's about setting achievable goals, establishing supportive routines and habits, building resilience against distractions, and practising self-compassion and flexibility. Through these practices, you can develop the discipline necessary to navigate the digital world without losing sight of your goals, ultimately leading to greater productivity, fulfillment, and success in your personal and professional life.

8

Conclusion: Embracing a Balanced Digital Life

This chapter serves as a reflective pause, summarizing key insights and lessons from the book, and more importantly, it stands as a beacon of motivation for readers to integrate these learnings into their lives. As we traverse through this final chapter, we reiterate the central theme that has been a recurrent echo throughout the book – the pursuit of balance in our digital engagements and the art of mindful technology use.

The digital age has unfurled a world of unprecedented connectivity and information access, transforming every facet of our lives. While it has ushered in remarkable advancements and conveniences, it has also presented unique challenges – blurring lines between work and personal life, the constant barrage of digital distractions, and the subtle erosion of our offline interactions. This book has been a guide, a companion in navigating these challenges, offering strategies and insights to harness the power of technology responsibly and mindfully.

In the initial chapters, we delved into the complex dynamics of digital distractions and temptations. We unraveled why our brains are magnetically drawn to these digital interruptions and how they can derail our focus and productivity. The first critical step was understanding the psychology behind digital temptations, including the concept of instant gratification and the dopamine-driven feedback loops created by social media and other digital platforms. This knowledge equipped us with the tools to develop effective strategies to resist and overcome the allure of digital distractions, setting the foundation for a disciplined and focused approach to technology use.

As we progressed, the book highlighted the importance of nurturing offline relationships and fostering real-world connections. In an era where digital communication often overshadows face-to-face interaction, we emphasized the unique value and irreplaceable depth that in-person connections bring to our lives. We explored how offline friendships, family time, community involvement, and social responsibility enrich our emotional well-being and contribute to our sense of belonging and purpose. These chapters served as a reminder of the fundamental human need for direct, personal interaction and the profound benefits of engaging in our communities and building solid and meaningful relationships outside the digital realm.

The journey then steered us towards the vital aspect of self-discipline in the context of ubiquitous digital distractions. We examined various techniques and strategies, such as the Pomodoro Technique, time-blocking, and focus-enhancing tools, that enhance concentration and minimise distractions. The book underscored the significance of creating a conducive environment for focus, setting clear boundaries for technology use, and integrating mindfulness and meditation practices to bolster our attention and concentration. Building and maintaining self-discipline routines emerged as a critical theme, highlighting the role of routine and habit formation in fostering self-discipline and the importance of resilience against distractions.

As we conclude, it's time to weave together these insights and strategies into a cohesive tapestry. "Embracing a Balanced Digital Life" is a summary of what has been discussed and a call to action. It invites readers to reflect on their digital habits, reassess their relationship with technology, and embark on a path towards a more balanced, mindful, and fulfilling digital existence. This chapter aims to inspire readers to apply the principles and strategies explored throughout the book, encouraging them to cultivate a digital life that harmonizes with their personal and professional aspirations.

The message of balance and mindful technology use that resonates through the pages of this book is more than a mere concept; it's a practical, achievable goal. It's about using technology as a tool to enhance our lives, not as a distraction that detracts from it. It's about recognizing the value of unplugging, connecting with others in the real world, and being present at the moment. It's about taking control of our digital interactions, making conscious choices, and setting boundaries to ensure our engagement with technology remains healthy, positive, and enriching.

In this final chapter, we recapitulate the main points discussed and reinforce the overarching theme of finding equilibrium in our digital interactions. We encourage readers to embrace a balanced digital life – where technology serves as a bridge to our goals and aspirations, not a barrier. As we conclude this journey, we hope that the insights and strategies presented will guide readers to navigate their digital world with intentionality, mindfulness, and a renewed sense of purpose.

The Importance of Mindful Technology Use

In the concluding reflections of our journey, a vital theme emerges with resounding clarity: the importance of mindful technology use. This final contemplation is not merely a recapitulation but a reinforcement of a critical concept - the intentional and conscious use of digital tools. Here, we emphasize how mindful engagement with technology can significantly enhance personal and professional productivity, bolster mental health, and enrich relationships. This narrative also revisits strategies for resisting the pervasive allure of digital temptations, advocating for a more controlled and conscious digital life.

Mindful Technology Use: A Cornerstone for Modern Living

In an age where digital devices are interwoven into the fabric of our daily lives, using technology mindfully has become indispensable. Mindful technology use implies an intentional and focused interaction with digital tools, ensuring that these tools serve us, rather than us becoming subservient to them. It's about using technology with purpose and deliberation rather than as a default reaction to boredom or a habitual escape from reality.

Enhancing Personal and Professional Productivity

One of the most tangible benefits of mindful technology use is the enhancement of personal and professional productivity. When used mindfully in the professional realm, technology becomes a powerful ally. It can streamline workflows, automate mundane tasks, and facilitate seamless communication. However, when used indiscriminately, it can become a source of endless distraction. Mindful use of technology in professional settings involves setting clear boundaries - designated times for checking emails, scheduling specific periods for deep work, and using productivity apps to prioritise tasks.

In our personal lives, mindful technology can help us reclaim time and focus on activities that truly matter. It enables us to engage in meaningful pursuits – be it hobbies, learning new skills, or simply unwinding with a good book – without the constant interruptions of digital notifications.

Improving Mental Health

The impact of technology on mental health is a topic of increasing concern. Constant connectivity and the overwhelming influx of information can lead to stress, anxiety, and a feeling of being perpetually behind. Mindful technology use advocates for a balanced approach - engaging with digital tools in a way that doesn't detract from mental well-being. This involves recognizing and avoiding digital content that triggers negative emotions, setting aside time to unplug and disconnect, and using technology to access resources that promote mental health, such as meditation apps or online counseling services.

Moreover, mindful technology use entails being present in our online and offline interactions. It encourages us to engage with digital media consciously and reflectively rather than passively consuming content that adds little value to our lives.

Enriching Relationships

In the realm of personal relationships, the role of technology is a double-edged sword. While it can connect us with friends and family across distances, it can also create a sense of disconnection and alienation when used excessively or inappropriately. Mindful technology use in relationships means being present and attentive in our interactions with others, free from the distractions of our digital devices. It involves using technology to enhance relationships – planning meet-ups, sharing experiences, and staying connected – while recognizing the importance of face-to-face interactions and the unique depth they bring to our relationships.

Strategies for Resisting Digital Temptations

Throughout this book, we've explored various strategies for resisting digital temptations and distractions. These include setting specific goals for technology use, establishing tech-free zones and times, and using apps that monitor and limit our digital consumption. We've delved into techniques like the Pomodoro Technique for managing time and focus and the role of mindfulness practices in enhancing our awareness and control over our digital habits.

Fostering a Conscious and Controlled Digital Life

The essence of fostering a conscious and controlled digital life lies in making deliberate choices about how we interact with technology. It's about recognizing when digital tools enhance our lives and when they detract from it. This conscious approach to technology use requires continuous effort and vigilance but pays dividends through increased productivity, improved mental health, and more prosperous relationships.

As we conclude, the message is clear and compelling: embrace technology mindfully and with intention. Let us use digital tools to enrich our lives, not to overshadow them. By practising mindful technology use, we can navigate the digital world with discernment and control, ensuring that our engagement with technology remains balanced, healthy, and harmonious with our overall life goals.

Fostering Real-World Connections and Community Engagement

In the digital era, where virtual interactions often dominate our social landscape, fostering real-world connections and community engagement emerges as an essential counterbalance. This chapter revisits and underscores the profound value of nurturing offline relationships – a theme that resonates deeply throughout the book. Here, we delve into the myriad ways real-world connections enhance our well-being, discussing the significance of building and maintaining friendships outside the digital realm, the irreplaceable worth of face-to-face interactions, and the myriad benefits that stem from active participation in community activities and volunteer work.

The Essentiality of Offline Relationships

Our journey through the digital age underscores a crucial truth: despite the convenience and breadth of online connections, they cannot wholly replace the depth and richness of offline relationships. Face-to-face interactions carry many subtle cues – tone of voice, body language, facial expressions –fundamental to building strong, empathetic, and understanding relationships. These nuances of in-person communication foster deeper connections, aiding in developing trust and emotional bonds that are less easily forged through digital means.

Offline relationships also play a pivotal role in our emotional and psychological health. Engaging with friends, family, and acquaintances in the physical world fulfils our inherent need for social connection and belonging, which is only partially satisfied by online interactions. These real-world connections provide support, joy, and comfort, significantly impacting our well-being and life satisfaction.

Building and Maintaining Friendships in the Real World

The art of building and maintaining friendships in the real world involves a conscious effort to nurture these connections. The book explores various avenues and strategies for developing offline friendships. One key aspect is the active pursuit of shared interests and activities. Joining clubs and groups or engaging in community activities provides fertile ground for meeting people with similar interests and forging new friendships.

Maintaining these friendships requires continuous effort. Regular meet-ups, whether for coffee, a meal, or a shared activity, are crucial.

These consistent interactions help solidify the bonds of friendship, allowing them to grow and evolve. The book also highlights the importance of quality over quantity in companies. Deep, meaningful relationships are often more fulfilling and supportive than a more significant number of superficial connections.

The Importance of Face-to-Face Interactions

Face-to-face interactions are unparalleled in conveying empathy, emotion, and subtlety. The book emphasizes that while digital communication is invaluable for maintaining long-distance relationships or for convenient quick exchanges, in-person interactions truly deepen and enrich relationships.

Engaging in face-to-face conversations allows for fully expressing and interpreting emotions, fostering a more profound understanding between individuals. It also enables more effective conflict resolution, as nuances are less likely to be misunderstood, and empathy is more easily conveyed and perceived. Additionally, physical presence in interactions adds a dimension of shared experiences and memories, further strengthening individual bonds.

Participating in Community Activities and Volunteer Work

Community engagement and volunteer work are highlighted in the book as powerful means of connecting with others while contributing positively to society. These activities provide a sense of purpose and fulfilment that extends beyond personal gains. By participating in community projects, local events, or volunteer opportunities, individuals contribute to the betterment of their communities and build a sense of belonging and connectedness.

Volunteering, in particular, is a profound way to meet diverse groups of people, develop new skills, and gain unique experiences. It fosters a sense of altruism and empathy as individuals work towards common goals for the greater good. Community involvement also provides a platform for civic engagement and social change, allowing individuals to actively shape their societal landscape.

The Interplay of Digital and Real-World Connections

The book does not advocate for a complete disconnection from the digital world but emphasizes a balanced approach. Digital tools and platforms can be instrumental in facilitating and enhancing real-world connections. For instance, social media can organize and coordinate face-to-face meet-ups or community events. The key is to use these digital tools to enrich and not replace direct human interactions.

In our digitally-dominated era, the value of fostering real-world connections and community engagement cannot be overstated. These offline relationships and interactions are crucial to our emotional well-being, providing a sense of belonging, purpose, and fulfilment essential to our holistic well-being. By actively seeking and nurturing these connections, participating in community activities, and balancing our digital and real-world interactions, we can lead more enriched, balanced, and fulfilling lives. This chapter, and indeed the entire book, serves as a guide and a reminder of the enduring importance of direct human connections in an increasingly virtual world.

Developing Self-Discipline in a Distracted World

In an age where our attention is incessantly besieged by digital stimuli, the cultivation of self-discipline emerges as an essential skill for navigating this landscape of constant interruptions. The ability to maintain focus and productivity amidst a sea of digital distractions is not just advantageous; it's imperative for our personal and professional growth. This section recaps the vital role of self-discipline and summarizes the array of strategies and techniques outlined in the book to bolster concentration and focus.

The Vital Role of Self-Discipline

Self-discipline in a digitally saturated world is akin to steering a ship through turbulent waters. The sheer volume of distractions that digital technology presents – from the endless scroll of social media to the persistent buzz of notifications – can fragment our attention and diminish our productivity. Developing self-discipline is about regaining control over our attention and focus, enabling us to direct our energies towards tasks and goals that are truly meaningful and rewarding.

Enhancing Focus through Proven Techniques

1. **The Pomodoro Technique**: This time management method involves breaking down work into intervals (typically 25 minutes), separated by short breaks. Each interval, known as a 'Pomodoro', is a dedicated focus session where one works on a task without interruption. After each Pomodoro, a short break follows, allowing the mind to rest before the next focused session. This technique helps in maintaining high levels of concentration while preventing burnout.

2. **Time-Blocking**: Time-blocking is a scheduling method where specific blocks of time are allocated to given tasks or activities. This approach not only organizes the day but also sets clear boundaries for focused work, reducing the likelihood of being sidetracked by digital distractions. By dedicating specific periods to tasks, we can immerse ourselves more deeply in our work, enhancing productivity and efficiency.

3. **Creating a Conducive Environment for Concentration**: The environment in which we work significantly influences our ability to focus. The book emphasizes creating a workspace that minimizes distractions and is conducive to concentration. This can involve decluttering the work area, using noise-cancellation headphones in noisy environments, or setting up a dedicated workspace free from the usual home distractions.

Setting Achievable Goals and Forming Routines

1. **Goal Setting**: Setting clear, achievable goals is a foundational step in cultivating self-discipline. Goals

provide direction and a sense of purpose, making it easier to stay focused and motivated. The book highlights the importance of setting SMART (Specific, Measurable, Achievable, Relevant, Time-bound) goals that provide a clear roadmap for our efforts.

2. **Routine and Habit Formation**: Building routines and forming habits are crucial in embedding self-discipline into our daily lives. Routines create a structure that guides our daily actions, reducing the mental load of making constant decisions. Habit formation, on the other hand, automates certain behaviors, making it easier to adhere to our discipline practices without expending excessive willpower.

The Need for Self-Compassion and Flexibility

An often-overlooked aspect of developing self-discipline is the need for self-compassion and flexibility. The journey towards disciplined living is not devoid of setbacks and challenges. The book encourages readers to approach these hurdles with self-compassion, understanding that lapses are part of the learning process. Being flexible and adapting our routines and strategies in the face of changing circumstances or unexpected challenges is also vital. This adaptability ensures that our pursuit of self-discipline is sustainable and aligned with our evolving personal and professional lives.

Developing self-discipline in a distracted world is an ongoing process that requires commitment, effort, and a strategic approach. By employing techniques like the Pomodoro Technique and time-blocking, creating environments conducive to focus, setting achievable goals, building routines, and maintaining self-compassion and flexibility, we can effectively navigate the digital world. These practices empower us to reclaim our focus and direct it towards tasks and goals that are truly significant, ultimately leading to a more productive, fulfilling, and balanced life.

Embracing a Balanced Digital Life

As we draw the curtains on this insightful exploration of navigating the digital world, the overarching message that resonates is the significance of embracing a balanced digital life. This concluding section underlines the essence of finding harmony between our digital and real-world interactions. The digital age, with all its advancements and conveniences, has brought about profound changes in the way we communicate, work, and live. However, it's imperative to use these digital tools to our advantage, ensuring they enhance rather than detract from the quality of our lives.

The Harmony Between Digital and Real-World Interactions

Finding balance in our digital life means establishing a harmony between online and offline worlds. It involves recognizing the value and utility of digital tools while being mindful of their potential to consume excessive amounts of our time and attention. This balance is crucial in preventing the feeling of being overwhelmed and distracted, which often accompanies excessive digital use.

Digital tools, when used judiciously, can significantly enhance our productivity, broaden our knowledge, and keep us connected with those who matter. However, the real essence of life – the emotional connections, the physical experiences, and the unplugged moments of reflection – still lies predominantly in the real world. The art of balancing involves leveraging the benefits of the digital world without losing sight of the enriching experiences the physical world offers.

Using Digital Tools to Our Advantage

Using digital tools to our advantage requires a conscious and deliberate approach. It involves harnessing these tools to streamline our work, enhance our learning, and maintain connections while setting boundaries to prevent overuse. Practical strategies like setting specific times for checking emails and social media, using productivity apps, and employing digital wellness tools can help manage our digital consumption.

However, it's also about the mindful consumption of digital content – choosing quality over quantity, engaging with content that adds value to our lives, and avoiding the mindless scrolling that often leads to digital fatigue.

Not Letting Digital Tools Overpower Our Lives

A crucial aspect of maintaining a balanced digital life is ensuring that these tools do not overpower our lives. It's about not letting digital interactions take precedence over face-to-face conversations, not allowing screens to disrupt our sleep, and not permitting online activities to infringe upon the time reserved for offline hobbies and relaxation.

To prevent this overpowering, it's essential to cultivate periods of digital disconnection. Unplugging regularly, whether for a few hours each day or a designated digital detox day, can provide much-needed breaks from the constant connectivity, allowing us to recharge and refocus.

Cultivating a Healthier Digital Existence

The journey to a healthier, more balanced digital existence is ongoing and evolving. As the digital landscape changes, so too must our engaging strategies. This journey is about constant learning and adaptation, finding what works for us as individuals, and being open to changing our digital habits as our lives evolve.

Readers are encouraged to apply the principles and strategies discussed throughout the book to their own lives. This application is not about rigid adherence to a set of rules but about developing a personal understanding of how digital tools fit into our lives in a healthy, balanced way.

In embracing a balanced digital life, we open ourselves to a world where technology is a tool for enhancement, not a source of constant distraction. It's a world where our digital interactions complement, not replace, our real-world experiences. By applying the principles of mindful technology use, fostering real-world connections, developing self-discipline, and finding harmony between our digital and offline lives, we can cultivate a digital existence that is fulfilling, enriching, and in tune with our overall well-being. This balanced approach is beneficial for our personal and professional growth and essential for our mental and emotional health in the digital age.

About the Author

-106-

Ethan Ray is a thought leader in digital mindfulness and a champion for balanced living in the technology age. With a background in behavioural psychology, Ethan has dedicated his career to understanding the intersection between human behaviour and digital consumption. His insights into digital wellness have positioned him as a sought-after speaker and consultant, where he advises on creating environments that foster productivity and well-being.

www.ingramcontent.com/pod-product-compliance
Lightning Source LLC
Chambersburg PA
CBHW051439140726
47987CB00006B/2451